MARK BICKLEY

Also by Trevor Gill

The World on my Shoulders:
The Dean Lukin Story (1985)

South Australians:
Profiles of People and Places (1986)

MARK BICKLEY

a biography by TREVOR GILL

HarperSports
An imprint of HarperCollins*Publishers*

Quote from *My Life* by Tony Lockett used with permission of
Pan Macmillan Publishers

Harper*Sports*
An imprint of HarperCollins*Publishers*, Australia

First published in Australia in 2001
Reprinted in 2001
by HarperCollins*Publishers* Pty Limited
ABN 36 009 913 517
A member of the HarperCollins*Publishers* (Australia) Pty Limited Group
www.harpercollins.com.au

Copyright © Australian Sports Professionals Pty Ltd 2001

The right of Trevor Gill to be identified as the moral rights author
of this work has been asserted by him in accordance with the *Copyright
Amendment (Moral Rights) Act 2000* (Cth).

This book is copyright.
Apart from any fair dealing for the purposes of private study, research
criticism or review, as permitted under the Copyright Act, no part may
be reproduced by any process without written permission.
Inquiries should be addressed to the publishers.

HarperCollins*Publishers*
25 Ryde Road, Pymble, Sydney, NSW 2073, Australia
31 View Road, Glenfield, Auckland 10, New Zealand
77–85 Fulham Palace Road, London W6 8JB, United Kingdom
Hazelton Lanes, 55 Avenue Road, Suite 2900, Toronto, Ontario M5R 3L2
and 1995 Markham Road, Scarborough, Ontario M1B 5M8, Canada
10 East 53rd Street, New York, NY 10022, USA

National Library of Australia Cataloguing-in-Publication data:

Gill, Trevor, 1953– .
 Mark bickley: a biography.
 ISBN 978 0 7322 6844 2.
 1. Bickley, Mark. 2. Australian football players – South
 Australia – Biography. 3. Australian football – South
 Australia. I. Title.
796.336092

Cover design by Luke Causby, HarperCollins Design Studio
Cover photograph used courtesy of Allsport

CONTENTS

Acknowledgments		ix
Foreword by Stephen Kernahan		xi
Introduction		1
1	A True Champion	5
2	A Footy Family	9
3	A Boom Recruit	22
4	Highs and Lows	27
5	Juggling Commitments	44
6	Walking on Fire	49
7	The Modra Phenomenon	56
8	A Defining Year	69
9	Diary of Disaster	73
10	Wilderness Years	89
11	A Club in Transition	103
12	Injury and Courage	112
13	Blight Takes the Helm	118
14	Fulfilling a Dream	127
15	The Famous Number 18	131
16	A Football Life	137
17	Against the Odds	144
18	The Pinnacle	152
19	Triumph and Reflection	163
20	Onwards and Upwards	169
21	And Again?	174
22	Soldiering On	191
23	A New Coach, a New Start	198
24	The Right Time	208
25	Back from the Brink	214

DEDICATION

This book traces my life to date and the many challenges and joys that I have experienced in my football career.

As I grow older, I will reflect with increasing pride on my involvement in football at the highest level with team mates, coaches and a club that showed faith in me and allowed me to fulfil my ambitions in the game. It has been an honour to play for and captain the Adelaide Football Club.

From the outset in Port Pirie, I had enormous support and encouragement from my parents, Max and Babs. Later, I found a very special person who, through all of the moods, injuries, absence and impositions that come with the game, has stood by me in good times and bad. My wife, Tanya, has been patient, tolerant, understanding and selfless. Without her, I could not have achieved what I have in football and in life. I must acknowledge the tremendous support of Tanya's parents Margaret and Rod Kuchel.

Our beautiful daughters – Shayne, Natasha and Aleesha – are my pride and joy. Through all the demands and pressures of life, the unconditional and complete love of children maintains your perspective, as well as providing endless hours of pleasure watching them grow and develop. I believe my greatest challenges are still to come – both in football and in life – and I look forward to meeting both with great effort and enthusiasm. If nothing else, football has taught me that there is no substitute for hard work, and that persistence does pay.

MARK BICKLEY

ACKNOWLEDGMENTS

When I was approached by Mark Bickley to write this book, I could not have imagined the level of support and cooperation that it would generate.

Former and current coaches, team mates and people associated with Mark were so willing to contribute. I would particularly like to thank John Reid, Graham Cornes, Robert Shaw, Malcolm Blight, Gary Ayres and Stephen Kernahan for their willingness to talk to me about Mark. It is a show of the respect with which he is held in that company.

Without the warm welcome and help of Max and Babs Bickley in Port Pirie, I would not have been able to delve into Mark's childhood and look at the competitive spirit that had its origins in backyard footy and cricket games with his brother David and his mates. Babs has a suitcase full of newspaper clippings from Mark and David's earliest days in the game. It was a rich resource that I visited often.

I also acknowledge the assistance of the Adelaide Football Club and News Limited and thank Ian Gray, Mark's manager for his support, along with the encouragement and professionalism of Alison Urquhart and Veronica Miller of HarperCollins*Publishers*.

This story required many hours of taped interviews. The word processing of those tapes into transcribed pages was prompt and professional with the support of Jackie Cullum and Mary Stephens. Without them, I could not have met the deadline. I also sincerely thank my wife Shirley and children – Tim, Robert, Alice and James – for enduring the pressure of that deadline.

Finally, I thank Mark and Tanya Bickley. Working with them has been a pleasure.

TREVOR GILL

FOREWORD

There is no greater feeling than being the first player to hold the AFL premiership cup after winning a grand final. It is the privileged position of the captain. Hoisting that cup is the primary objective of every footballer. In those fleeting moments of immense pride and satisfaction, you fulfil career ambitions, reward sacrifices, and begin to celebrate an impossible dream with team mates who will be friends for life.

In 1997, Mark Bickley was captain of the Adelaide Football Club when it won its first AFL premiership. And he did it again the following year. It was a remarkable individual and team achievement.

Mark Bickley's life story, and his rise to the peak of football glory, is about an unswerving desire to succeed. He did it through sheer hard work, commitment and unquestioned loyalty to his ideals, and to those of his club. The fact that he did it against the odds is inspirational.

Firstly, he had to make the transition from country player to league footballer in Adelaide. Then in 1990, as the Adelaide Football Club was preparing for its first season in the AFL, he forced his way into the squad almost entirely on the basis of his work ethic. Mark states he was the last player to be picked in the Crows' inaugural squad. By round four of the club's first season in 1991, he was in the team, and there he stayed. Mark later captained the side as he played – tough, fearless, tenacious and reliable, a footballer who runs through the lines. A leader.

My first memories of Mark were playing for South Australia in the early 1990s. I played a lot of State football with mates like Chris McDermott, Tony McGuinness, John Platten and Craig Bradley – each of whom were outstanding footballers. After the arrival of the Crows, there was an influx of younger players into the South Australian side, among them Mark Bickley. Once again, he was not an automatic selection. He simply worked his backside off to get into the team and he quickly cemented his place. I was immediately impressed at Mark's ability to get a roll on an opposition player, negating him, then finding the ball himself. I gained a lot of enjoyment from being his team mate.

He has always loved playing the game, like a kid with his first footy. This book explains how Mark's lifelong passion with the game had its origins in the Solomontown Football Club in country South Australia, how he rose through the ranks of South Australia's first AFL team, and how he plays on with distinction and endurance – almost the last standing from the Adelaide Football Club's first squad.

Mark Bickley's gallant football record speaks for itself:

- Won the Madigan Medal in South Australia's tough Spencer Gulf League in 1988
- Recruited to South Adelaide in 1988
- Member of the Adelaide Football Club's inaugural squad in 1990
- AFL debut against Essendon, 13 April 1991
- 228 AFL games to the end of 2001

- Captain of the Adelaide Football Club 1997 to 2000, including premiership captain in 1997 and 1998
- Adelaide Football Club Best Team Man Awards in 1992, 1993 and 2000
- Played for South Australia seven times

It is a privilege to be asked to write this foreword to the biography of Mark Bickley, a very special footballer, a great bloke and a proud family man. It is a story that should inspire every footballer at every level – indeed every person – because it proves that the harvest of hard work, honesty and commitment is success.

When Mark does finally hang up his boots, he will be able to sit back and reflect on a magnificent career as a player, and one that should lay the foundations for some exciting involvement in the future of the great Australian game.

STEVE KERNAHAN

Stephen Kernahan played 136 games for Glenelg in the South Australian National Football League between 1981 and 1985, starring in the grand final victory in his final year at the club. He was recruited by Carlton at the end of 1985 and played 251 games for the club, captaining the side for a record 226 games from 1986 to 1997, including premierships in 1987 and 1995. He was Carlton's leading goalkicker for eleven successive seasons and was selected in All Australian teams in 1985, 1986, 1987, 1988, 1989, 1990, 1992 and 1994. Stephen Kernahan played 13 State of Origin games for South Australia. He is Chairman of Selectors and an assistant coach with Carlton.

INTRODUCTION

This is a narrative about Mark Bickley, a remarkable individual. But, in every turn of phrase, in every emphasis and in its ultimate conclusion, the intention of this book is to present him as a member of a team. If an attempt was made at anything but, the subject would have walked away before the first sod of the story was turned. 'Team' is the emblem Mark Bickley wears beyond anything else. His milestones are marked with the word 'we'.

Individual sporting achievements have pride of place in this nation's character. Championship golfers kiss cups and their caddies. World-beating swimmers greet the national anthem with one hand over their heart and another around a toy koala. Grand Slam tennis players scale courtside peaks of people and fall into emotional embraces. Olympic gold-medallists slump at the end of their tracks, having taken on the world and won, then find themselves numbed and bewildered about what to do next. The fairest and best players in Australian football, known as Brownlow Medallists, are driven around an emotion-filled stadium to be honoured by almost 100 000 people who may not necessarily barrack for them. In each case, there are glorious, spontaneous, slow-motion moments of individual acknowledgment, wonderment and elation. But when the stardust settles, every one of those champions accepts that nothing would have been possible without the support of a team, whether it be teammates, coach, family or, paradoxically, demons.

At the nerve edges of elite sport, there are feats and retreats. Some athletes seek to escape from their own triumphs and, instead, search for an afterlife, or the life they sacrificed to become a legend. Olympic history, some of it very recent, emphasises this truth. Some champions are haunted for the rest of their lives by failure to claim their sport's ultimate prize, whether it be an Olympic medal, or a football premiership. Tony Lockett, the sensational spearhead of St Kilda and Sydney, the greatest goalkicker in the history of the Australian Football League and a winner of the game's highest individual honour, a Brownlow Medal, told of his despair and regret in retirement over not being able to win a premiership in 17 winters. Garry Lyon, the former Melbourne champion, once said that the AFL grand final week was a time of unhappiness for him. He told Mark Bickley about a sick feeling in his stomach, knowing he would go through life without experiencing a premiership.

Mark Bickley feared his football life would be unfulfilled. If it is possible to extract an ounce of self-interest from him, this would be it. This would be something he'd have to endure on his own. Mark's first experience of a football club was in nappies and a stroller. From sliding across the polished floor of the Solomontown Football Club in flannelette pyjamas and dressing gown to his first guernsey and baggy shorts, he yearned for little other than football. He cried when the coach refused to play him because he was not old enough. When he did play, the game embraced him, not in the privileged manner of some God-given skill, but by a determination driven by something within him. When he became an AFL footballer, the quest for the ultimate prize had a constant companion: the fear that he would not achieve it. In 1993, three years into his journey,

Adelaide was one game from a grand final. The team dominated this game, but did not know how to win it. As a result, the club floundered and, in the four years of turmoil that followed, Mark lost faith at times. In 1996 he felt there was no light at the end of the tunnel. He was reaching his late 20s, and he started to wonder if he would ever play finals football again. 'In my heart of hearts, I didn't believe I would play in a grand final. I am sure some of the other players felt the same way, and it hurt.'

Of course, ultimate success in team sport is not something an individual can control. Mark recognises that you can contribute, though. He refers to players such as Tony Lockett, Gary Ablett, Garry Lyon and Paul Roos. 'Despite their greatness, they couldn't do it alone, and I feel for them. There are times when a special group of players get it right, and the chemistry happens – that is the wonderful thing about team sport. Individual awards are important in the context of contribution to the team. I recognise and admire personal achievement, but when people offer their congratulations, they don't actually know what the person is feeling. They cannot see their innermost thoughts.

'Success as a team is something entirely different. You can look your teammate in the eye and know he is experiencing exactly the same emotions as you are. It is something you share forever. Having worked so hard as a group, supporting each other when times get tough, you enjoy success with absolute certainty that your teammates feel exactly the same way. Time will never fade the memories.'

1
A TRUE CHAMPION

In the long shadows at the MCG on Saturday, 27 September 1997, Mark Bickley and his teammates elevated themselves into AFL history. In the immediate aftermath of the Adelaide Football Club's first premiership win, they experienced what their coach told them would be an extraordinary adrenalin rush and an outburst of unrestrained emotion. For several minutes in the groundswell of relief and realisation, they embraced each other, tumbled over each other, cried on each other's shoulders and laughed at each other's tears. For more than two hours, almost 100 000 people – and who knows how many beyond – had witnessed in roaring crescendos, moaning despair and vacuumed silence the game's ultimate contest between a club that had not won an AFL premiership in its seven-year history, and another – St Kilda – that had claimed just one in a century of endeavour.

Yet, in those fleeting, free-falling moments after the final siren, it was as if nobody else was there for the Adelaide players. It was just them, cocooned in their own destiny, tumbling about like kids let out to play. Kids forever.

Mark was one of the original players selected in an Adelaide Football Club squad assembled in haste. He was called up mainly for the purposes of equity, representing an unfashionable and struggling South Australian National Football League club. This club needed to be represented in a team purported to be for all South Australians. Truthfully, he was probably an afterthought. Within four weeks of the club's first AFL season in 1991, he was in the team and, except for injury, he was never overlooked for selection.

Very early, the club recognised that he was a player who would not be denied his ambition. Driven more by determination than skill, he rose to become the club's first premiership captain. He rose to win three Best Team Man awards. He rose to become a champion. He rose to become one of the privileged few to hold aloft a Premiership Cup as captain. He rose to do it twice, joining the ranks of post World War II leaders like Wayne Carey, Stephen Kernahan, John Worsfold, Michael Tuck, Terry Daniher, Mike Fitzpatrick, Don Scott, Royce Hart, John Nicholls, Ron Barassi, John Beckwith, Noel McMahan, Fred Flanagan and Dick Reynolds.

Early in 1997, in his first year as coach of the Adelaide Football Club, Malcolm Blight kept reassuring his players that if they played his way, they would succeed. 'Just stick with it,' he urged. 'I know that it works.'

Persistence is also a strong feature of Mark Bickley's character. His theory was always that if he trained his hardest, did everything right and set himself goals, his turn would come. 'Sometimes,' he says, 'things don't happen for you, and you begin to lose faith. But you've got to hang in there, and success will eventually come. It comes when you start believing in yourself and your teammates.' To win three finals on the way to the ultimate showdown, including a memorable two-point victory over the Western Bulldogs after trailing by 31 points at half-time, demonstrated that the Crows believed in themselves. To come from twelfth to top was an emphatic reflection of self-belief.

'I was there at the birth of the club, and saw it evolve so much through coaches and players. In those minutes after the final siren against St Kilda, I went to every player. Some of us had been together for years, some had played only a handful of games. But there was a special bond between us. I was ecstatic for the people within the club – people who had worked so hard to form a club from nothing. I felt so much pleasure at seeing what it meant to others.'

Before the 1997 grand final, Mark and his wife, Tanya, had seen the hit movie *Titanic*, and he had been moved by the scene when Leonardo DiCaprio and Kate Winslet stand on the bow of the ship, moon on the water, wind in their hair, almost flying above the icy waves. As the Crows players swarmed in celebration after the final siren at the MCG, David Pittman grabbed Mark around the hips and lifted him high in the air above a pack of photographers and journalists. Arms outstretched, he immediately recalled the cameo scene from *Titanic*. 'I'm the king of the world,' he screamed. The microphones picked it up and, coming down from the emotion of the moment, he was acutely embarrassed. Here was a player who always put the team before himself.

Absolute elation and the reality of the achievement hit when the captain and coach lifted the trophy. In Mark's words, 'This is the crowning moment, the symbolic gesture, the time you are recognised as the champions. The roar of the crowd lifts you off your feet. It is an extraordinary feeling and a great honour to be there as captain when others could have done the job just as well. On the other hand, it is just a feeling of immense relief. It's like a mountain being taken off your shoulders.'

This was also new territory for Malcolm Blight, who had coached Geelong into three grand finals, without victory. Mark lifted the trophy with his right hand, and with the trophy between them, Blight reached across with his right. As a thousand flashbulbs recorded the moment for posterity, Blight's face was obscured by his arm.

'Later, I asked Blighty why he didn't grab the cup with his left hand. He said something like, "There's a good reason for that." I expected some profound statement, or perhaps a sign of superstition. But instead, he just looked at me and said "I didn't know what I was doing. I'd never been up there before, and it was all new to me." This cracked me up because Blighty was considered to be the guy who'd done everything, including winning two premierships with North Melbourne. But he wasn't captain and he didn't go up onto the dais to lift the cup with the coach, Ron Barassi. The only thing missing in Malcolm Blight's treasure chest had been a premiership as coach. We were happy to repay him for the knowledge he brought to the club.'

In the quiet afterglow of the Adelaide Football Club's triumph in 1997, Malcolm Blight took his captain aside and told him it would change his life. Mark asked him what he meant.

'Premiership captains don't come along every day,' Blight replied. 'It is a special honour. If you want to take up coaching, you can. If you want to comment on the game in the media, you can.'

The coach's words sank in. 'Those comments mean a lot to me now. Winning a premiership and being in the privileged position of captain does change your life. It has opened some doors for me, and I think I have gained respect from people who appreciate how hard it is to achieve this goal in life. Through it all, the thing I cherish most is being able to share the good times and the memories with people who will be my lifelong friends. I wouldn't swap my footy career for the world.

2
A FOOTY FAMILY

The Solomontown Football Club sits on the outskirts of town. The building is red brick; the club's colours are blue and white and the team known as The Cats. There is a distinct air of tradition in the clubroom. Old, rust-brown photographs hang on the walls. Velvet-based trophies sit heavily in cabinets and lace adorns the main table in front of the stage. The stage itself is clearly a place of consequence and ceremony, with the ornate curtains that drape like heavy jowls from the ceiling and the old piano that must have taken a half a team of footballers to heave into position. On most nights, an empty chair and small table stand on the stage, as if awaiting an occasion; such as for bingo once a week. Bingo survives in Port Pirie. So do betting shops, darts, eight ball tournaments, cribbage and crabbing competitions.

Most of the floor space inside the club is dedicated to dining tables and chairs. Somewhere is a kitchen where volunteers cook and wash dishes, and the bar is a curious mixture of old and new ... from heavy carved sherry decanters and thin engraved glasses on pretty doilies to blue and white stubby holders. Hanging from the ceiling in the middle of the room is a mirror ball, testimony to a disco scene that must have swirled with dancers on countless sweaty Saturday nights. A generation before that, it was dinner dances and basket suppers. One wonders how often the cloth is lifted off the piano these days, and for whom the ivories are tickled.

The Solomontown Football Club is a place for all people and all seasons. It is rich in its passing parade of characters, champions and tragedy. It's easy to raise a giggle over the memory of people such as Jackie Kerrin, who spent countless hours at the bar with his fox terrier dog. To ensure the dog was welcome in the club, Jackie made it a member and paid its subscription religiously each year. Every day, the dog dutifully sat on a rug in the corner. In 1962 Solomontown engaged a new coach, Danny O'Dea. He came from Whyalla with a big reputation, and a kelpie in his ute. Wherever Danny went, his dog followed. That is, until he walked into the club and was immediately spotted by Jackie Kerrin at the bar.

'That dog's not welcome in this bar unless he's a member,' Jackie said. 'Make him a member or show him the door.' The Solomontown Football Club soon had two four-legged members.

On a more serious note, the club solemnly commemorates the memory of a past player, Ray Rawlins. Ray was killed in 1959 when his utility rolled down an embankment onto a railway line on the way home from an end-of-season footy trip to Murray Bridge. The former champion footballer was only 26 when he left a widow and three young children. The Solomontown Football Club enveloped them in care.

The Solomontown Football Club had its origins in the early 1890s when there was a huge influx of people into Port Pirie seeking work at the new Broken Hill and Associated smelters. To cope with this growth in population, a community of men, women and children erected canvas, calico and hessian houses on the banks of Dead Horse Creek, just past the harbourmaster's office and near the entrance of the smelters. For this swampy, mosquito-ridden existence, they paid rent of one shilling a week and pioneered a spirit of endeavour, togetherness and pride that still binds the people of Port Pirie to a place of the working man and woman; a place of blue singlets and blouses.

The club is on a busy road which, in one direction, leads to an enchanting place called Crystal Brook, and in the other to the smelters, the smoking heartland and big pay packet of Port Pirie. Across the road from the club is the Globe Oval. Solid brick change rooms painted blue and white show how the club has advanced since the days when players had to strip in tumbledown stables at the rear of the Globe Hotel. Out the back of the Club is Solomontown Beach, a sandy shore and playground on the upper reaches of a muddy, mangrove-lined inlet of Spencer Gulf.

The huge chimney of the smelter, one of the highest stacks in the Southern Hemisphere, dominates the skyline of Port Pirie, dispersing gases emitted from the production of lead, zinc, gold, silver and copper. Travelling along the road from the Solomontown Football Club to the Pasminco Smelter is a step back in time. The route takes you past a fodder store selling turtle food and pig's ears; wooden fishing boats swinging on their moorings; the customs house, big corner hotels with wide balconies and curling patterns of wrought iron; the heavy facade of the Adelaide Steamship Company; and the Australian Workers' Union office. Apart from the imposing smelters, the blinding white grain silos on the wharves can be seen from all around, and hundreds of television antennas reach high above galvanised iron rooftops. In the shimmering distance, the Flinders Ranges rise in spectacular indigo peaks above the great Outback.

Port Pirie is a place of comings and goings. National Highway One flanks the city on its loop around the continent and big ships tie up at the wharves, escorted up and down the channel by the tugboats *Tanunda* and *Ungarra*. The town was once at the crossroads of the Commonwealth and State railways, the stopping place of legendary trains such as the Ghan and the Indian Pacific. That was before Pirie was bypassed. The 'Three Train Road' used to run opposite Solomontown School, reflecting the three gauges of track – narrow, standard and broad.

These lines of steel brought Barbara Evans to Pirie. It was 1952 when her father, a stationmaster, came to town with his family after postings in Penola, Canberra and Port Augusta. She met Max Bickley at primary school, tagging along with him and his mates, kicking up dust and footballs. Max was born in Port Pirie. His dad worked in the smelters and it was only natural that Max should follow him through the big gates.

Max played football for Solomontown and, when Barbara, or Babs as she became known, started to become a little more serious about stringing along with the tall, dark centre half forward, the club became their second home.

'It was so social, because in those days it was six o'clock closing in the hotels,' Babs recalls. 'When I first started going out with Max, we used to go to the Globe Hotel, which is now the Sportsman's Tavern, after games on Saturdays. At six o'clock, we'd go off to someone's house for a party. Then there was a period of planning and hard work, and the clubroom was built by volunteers. Solomontown footy club, or Sollys as we call it, then became the meeting place. In those days, we had cabarets and there was always fundraising. I was young and used to go down there in my netball uniform. Older ladies used to say, "Get out and sell raffle tickets!" So I used to sell the tickets. Then I thought I may as well join this ladies' committee. That was before I got married. I've been married 35 years and I have never been off the committee.'

Four teams played in the local football competition: Proprietary, Ports, Solomontown and Risdon. The rivalry was deadly, particularly between the blue and white of Solomontown and the green and white of Ports.

According to Babs, in the old days, quite a few of the Proprietary players were schoolteachers or policemen. The Catholics mainly played for Ports and the rest for Solomontown. Pirie was thriving, and many players couldn't get a game. Some went to Risdon, and some were on the fringes of the other teams.

Football and work were the main topics of conversation in most Port Pirie homes. While the rivalry was intense on the field, there was genuine friendship between the clubs and their players – and they played a lot of pranks on each other, too. One year before the finals, a group of Solomontown footballers ventured after dark deep into the backyards of Ports players and painted their chickens blue, seriously ruffling feathers behind enemy lines.

Max Bickley recalls how he knew everybody who played for the opposition and how friendly he was with them. 'You would go into a hotel, and if your friends from the opposition were there, you'd go up and talk to them. You still did all your social activities in your own rooms, but a lot of my best friends when I was growing up were playing for the opposition, and we used to go out together. I think it's because of the smallness of the town. That's how people became so close.' Over the years, league clubs in Adelaide, including South Adelaide, West Torrens and Norwood, tried to lure Max out of Pirie, but his bonds to the Solomontown Football Club were too strong, his roots too deeply entrenched in the smelters.

Besides, Max and Babs Bickley had a family to raise. Two boys – David and Mark. Before they could walk, the boys crawled around on the floor at the Solomontown Football Club, and when they could walk, they preferred to run.

The house at 2 Jenkins Street, Port Pirie is not exceptional. It is a modest home on a quarter-acre block. Max keeps the garden neat and tidy and Babs keeps the inside spotless. Having bought the place when they married, they've never shifted. Along one side of the house between the front fence and the almond tree is a wide, open area where some great 'Test' cricket matches were played. The first eight batsmen had to bat right handed, the last three left handed. The side fence was two, the back fence four, and over the fence into Mr Brittain's pumpkin patch was out. David Bickley was always David Hookes, Mark was always Greg Chappell. The dust of cover drives, scrambled singles and brilliant saves gave way to the mud and blood of football in winter. David was the former Sturt and Hawthorn champion Rick Davies. Mark, a one-eyed Port Adelaide supporter, was Russell Ebert, the Magpies' legendary four times Magarey Medallist.

Across the road was an open paddock where market gardens had once prospered. However, the block was sold, the glasshouses bulldozed and the dirt laced with shards of glass, which kept the kids at bay. So the Bickley backyard was Port Pirie's version of the MCG, balls thumping the side of the house and cockies sent out of the almond tree screeching in fear. The Aldridge brothers, Mark and Scott, were often seen with the Bickley boys. The four were similar in age, size, desire to win and willingness to have a go. Mick Lauritson, the butcher on the corner, would often hear the roars of triumph or the cries of pain drowning out his meat saw. On winter nights, after a bath and balm for the bruises and scratches, football was the main topic of conversation in the Bickley household. Max barracked for West Torrens, Babs for Glenelg. Her favourite player was Graham Cornes.

For the Bickley boys, sport was serious stuff. Mark, the younger of the two brothers, did not have it easy in the backyard. Much smaller than David, he often came out of the packs wiping tears from his cheeks, then diving back in for another go. Even as a six-year-old, fear was a thing to stare down.

'Even riding to school had its challenges. My brother and I would go past a big dog on our way to school. The dog used to bite me. Mum went around and asked the dog's owner to keep it in his yard, but he didn't. Dad taught me that dogs know when you are scared. I had to conquer that fear.'

It was Bob Boston who put Mark in a Port Adelaide guernsey. Bob was born in Rosewater, the heartland and breeding ground of the Port Adelaide Football Club. He played for Port at the end of the Fos Williams era in the early 1970s. When Fos had nothing more to prove at Port, he was enticed to coach at West Adelaide and Bob Boston followed like a disciple. After he retired from league football in Adelaide, Bob played for Solomontown, and he boarded with the Bickleys until he found his own house in Port Pirie. For years afterwards, Bob was a regular dinner guest in the Bickley house on Monday nights, and he would partner Mark in games of euchre around the kitchen table.

Bob instilled in Mark the Fos Williams gospel. He recognised that Mark had an unswerving desire to get the ball. The boy would also listen.

'Bob took an instant shine to the family atmosphere . . . and really took a special interest in [me],' Mark said. 'He used to tell us about Fos Williams. His passion for Port rubbed off on me. He would say things like, "If you haven't had a few stitches in your face and concussion by the time you're 18, then you're not going in hard enough." I remember getting a cut playing footy and pleading with Mum to take me to the doctor to put a stitch in it!

'In 1980 and 1981, Bob organised tickets and he took us to Adelaide to see Port win the Grand Final. After the game, he knew the doorman and took us into the change rooms. It was just amazing. I saw Russell Ebert, Greg Phillips, Max James, Brian Cunningham. Bob was talking to them, but because we were only young we didn't have a great deal to say. We were dumbstruck, and in awe of them all. We were really privileged. It really whet my appetite to play for Port Adelaide.'

Bob Boston recalls: 'Mark always had a complete honesty about him which shows in everything he does. At seven or eight, he held the floor in conversation with adults, and on the footy field he was fearless. I saw him play in a final at the age of 14, and marvelled at how he dominated the game from the centre with his attack on the ball and body. His strength always came from his hips and legs.'

Max Bickley, the quiet achiever, also kept an eye on his boys' progress in football. After retiring as a highly decorated player with Solomontown Football Club, Max successfully coached junior grades, until he stepped aside to manage the teams in which David and Mark played.

Max says he and his boys always discussed football. 'Mark was small, and I always used to tell him that if he went in hard for the ball, he wouldn't get hurt. I used to say, "If you sit out, you'll get pinged off as easy as anything."'

The wait for Mark's first real game of football for Solomotown was long and frustrating.

There was only one grade for the younger kids, the Under 13s. Often there would be boys of six or seven playing with 12-year-olds. Mark remembers how the competition was pretty uneven: 'I was about five and David was eight. He was playing in the Under 13s, and every week I'd get dressed up expecting to play. Mum and Dad had spoken to the coach, so I'd be allowed to run out and do the warm-up. But Mum told the coach not to put me on. It got to the last game of the year, the last quarter, the last five minutes. The coach had spent the season watching me cry after games because I hadn't played. I was shattered. Finally, he put me on for the last five minutes and the ball came straight to me. I got a kick and, of course, I was rapt. When the siren blew, I ran straight over to Mum, Dad and Bob Boston and said, "Did you see that, I got a kick!" Bob looked at me and said, "I didn't see you get a kick. All I saw was you skipping around with your jocks up your arse." So he called me "Skippy Pick Your Bum". Skippy has stuck as my nickname, but I'm quite happy to forget the rest of it.'

Mark was always competitive, according to his dad. 'You could tell, even when he was playing Under 13s, that he was going to be very good. Mark would be chasing a man, shepherding for someone else to have a kick, and running non-stop. You really have to push a lot of kids to get the most out of them, but you didn't have to do that with Mark. He just continually ran and did all the hard things. He was a bit ordinary with his kicking when he was young, but his hands were good.'

As often as possible, Max watched David and Mark play. He would listen to what their coaches had to say and only offered advice after a game if he saw something he didn't like.

'If ever I laid a head-high tackle or something like that Dad would say "Don't do that again or there will be big trouble," Mark said. 'As I grew older and started playing well, I was often targeted in games. I started to think that if I was getting whacked, I might try to whack a few guys back. I was very quickly sat down by Dad and told to get on with my footy and not be bothered about getting into blues.

'I loved my sport and all my growing up years in Port Pirie. I know that the freedom we had as kids was unrivalled. In school holidays, we'd ride to the creeks and go crabbing, go fishing or rabbiting or camping. We used to pitch a tent on someone's back lawn and sleep over. You could do everything – there were heaps of sports. We always had some sort of sporting practice every night of the week. I played cricket and tennis – the only sport I didn't play was soccer. But everything was available to us. If you liked it, you played it. We were just a bunch of guys getting around enjoying ourselves.'

Max Bickley was working at the smelters, but most people knew him through football – as a player or as a coach. As a young boy, Mark was asked by his teacher what he wanted to do when he grew up. He said he wanted to be a professional footballer. 'I don't know why I used to say that because I always believed that I would probably finish up working at the smelters with Dad. It's uncanny how I finished up doing both because my first job was as an apprentice electrician at the smelters.

'I vaguely remember Dad playing towards the end of his career. He has always been happiest when he's involved in footy. No matter what was happening at home or work, at 12 o'clock on a Saturday, he'd say, "Okay, we are going to the footy," and everything else was forgotten. After the game, we'd go straight to the clubrooms and get home late at night. Footy was a way of life.'

As early as Mark can remember, Babs was involved in Sollies. He can recall her hanging out guernseys for the A and B grade teams, or in the kitchen cooking all the teas after the game, or running raffles. The whole family was at the footy club. In fact, it wasn't just the Bickley family. Sollies drew in lots of families. Kids would be flying around on the floor in pyjamas and dressing gowns. Throughout his childhood, Mark's fondest memories were in some way tied up with the football club.

Every Sunday morning, Max used to say he was going to church. This was the name they gave to Sundays at the footy club. They'd have a few beers and play cards or cribbage. The players would have a 'hair of the dog' and talk about what happened the day before. David and Mark were a part of it all. They learned how to play cards at the club, euchre especially.

As he progressed through his early teens, Mark always found himself playing football against older opponents. Often he would play two games on a Saturday, willingly presenting himself for a more senior team in the afternoon after playing in the morning. At the age of 15, he was captain of the Under 16s. A year later, he was training with the A grade – elevating him into a team playing against men twice his age. It was 1986. David Bickley had already established himself in the side, having earned a formidable reputation as a key forward. In 1987, Mark played every A grade game. Solomontown played in the grand final against West Augusta. A gale forced the old Port Augusta grandstand to be evacuated halfway through the game and, for the first time, Mark suffered the gut-wrenching disappointment of losing a grand final at senior level. It had, however, been a defining year, as he had made the Spencer Gulf League Combined Side and North Adelaide Football Club expressed interest in the young centreman, who was starring in its country recruitment zone. Mark took a month off work to train with North Adelaide, but nobody at the club realised his potential, including its coach Mick Nunan, a former Port Pirie boy who had also played for Solomontown.

'There were two trial games, and after spending the first three quarters on the bench, they put me in the back pocket. I was frustrated by this – I had committed a month of my holidays from work to show North Adelaide what I could do as an on-baller, and I sat on my arse for most of the trial games before going into defence for a few minutes. Dad spoke to the club, but North could not guarantee me a full game. I decided to come home and play another season with Sollys. Besides, I had my apprenticeship at the smelters to think about.'

In 1988, Max Bickley was to be rewarded for his loyalty to Solomontown Football Club. That year also proved to be the springboard for one of football's great success stories.

After successfully coaching junior teams at Solomontown, Max was appointed A grade coach in 1988.

Max relished the senior coaching position at the club to which he had given long and loyal service. 'Mark had got his apprenticeship in the smelters and I used to take him to work every day. We'd talk football day in and day out. Once he got on the training track, you didn't have to worry about him. He just trained 100 per cent all of the time. David suffered from asthma and he didn't like training much. But once he was on the ground, he was brilliant, too. He would do everything right. Adelaide clubs chased David, but he didn't want to be a part of that scene. A lot of people who coach their sons get into them a bit, or favour them to the disadvantage of others. I was extremely proud to be coaching the two boys at senior level, but they were just members of the team.'

In 1988, Mark Bickley was the toast of the Spencer Gulf League, which is considered to be the toughest competition outside the South Australian National Football League.

Solomontown had a successful year. They won the premiership, their full forward, Larry Rawlins, son of Ray Rawlins, was the Spencer Gulf League's leading goalkicker. In 1988, Mark also won the Madigan Medal for the best and fairest player in the competition.

David was in the premiership team too, and he played an excellent game. It was a wonderful time for Mark, but his thoughts ultimately went beyond the local celebrations. 'It was fantastic. The whole family was involved. David and I played, Dad coached and Mum had been organising everything during the year. In one sense, it was the combination of what we had all set out to do. Probably from that point, I knew I had to move on because I really didn't think we could top what we had done that year. I was serving my apprenticeship as an electrician at the smelters and had money in my pocket, but I knew it was time to try the next level.' Mark made a commitment to himself to give it his best shot with North Adelaide. It was a daunting prospect for him to leave Port Pirie. Babs had always spoiled the Bickley boys. 'She's a very tidy and organised person. She even used to iron our underpants!' Mark says.

At the end of the 1988 season, Mark rang North Adelaide to tell them he was available to play, but that he needed to have his apprenticeship indentures transferred to Adelaide, and that he would need somewhere to live. North rang back and told him it would be difficult to find a job for a third-year apprentice in Adelaide and advised him to play another year in Port Pirie. Mark had tried twice to play with North Adelaide. He was, in fact, a little disappointed that Mick Nunan had not spoken to him considering his former relationship with the Solomontown Football Club.

A telephone call then came from South Adelaide Football Club stalwart Kevin 'Squizzy' Taylor. Mark told Kevin Taylor he was willing to play for South Adelaide, but that his primary concern was the transfer of his indentures for work. Within days, South Adelaide coach John Reid was on the Bickley family's doorstep, having driven to Port Pirie on the recommendation of South Augusta assistant coach David Shillabeer, who believed Mark had the potential to play league football.

Reid immediately recognised that Max and Babs Bickley were salt-of-the-earth people who had given Mark and his brother a good foundation in life. It was also apparent to Reid from that first meeting that Mark had the drive to succeed. Reid says, 'Having been out there and coached, I think there is a grassroots passion among country footballers that you don't necessarily get in a lot of city blokes. The city kids don't get it easy either, but in the bush you have to travel long distances and be prepared to give up a little more to play footy. If a talented country footballer comes to the city, and is prepared to give it an honest go, he is likely to succeed. I think it goes back to that passion and preparedness to work. I could see from the outset that Mark had all of those ingredients.'

Reid told the Bickley family that South Adelaide was struggling at the bottom of the league ladder and that the club was scouring the country for young players to 'give it a go'. Reid had coached South Augusta in 1981, so Babs and Max knew of him.

Two days later, Mark went for an interview with Mitsubishi Motors in Adelaide and within a week the company offered him a job. As things turned out, Mark Aldridge, who had played with David and Mark as kids, was also looking to play with South. He and Mark found a unit in Adelaide and moved in together. Mark recalls that South had to pay around $2000 to North Adelaide because he was in their zone, and that was the end of any relationship he might have had with that club.

3

A BOOM RECRUIT

A garden sprinkler provided Mark's wake-up call about the fitness level his new coach, John Reid, required. Having signed with South Adelaide, he was expected to attend training prior to Christmas, 1988. The first session involved a Sunday morning run. Mark had driven from Pirie the night before and decided to look around town, eventually finding his way to the Adelaide Casino. There, he found an old mate, 'Buck' Tully. After half a dozen schooners of beer, Mark then caught a taxi to a friend's house in North Adelaide, set the alarm, and crash-landed on the couch. Early the next morning, armed with a street directory, he set off for John Reid's home in the southern suburbs, where he was to meet with the South squad for a run. After drinking beer, it had not occurred to Mark to rehydrate with water.

It was 8.30 am and already 31 degrees. The squad had to run around a huge water catchment area, jumping about 25 fences over a distance of about 15 kilometres. Finally, they got to a drink station and Mark desperately reached for some water, only to have somebody accidentally knock the cup out of his hand.

Keen to impress, he didn't worry about the water and kept running. At about the 10-kilometre mark, he started to feel a bit sick. Then they came to the base of a steep hill. With about 500 metres to go to the finish, and trying to climb the hill, Mark was dizzy and could feel himself falling backwards. He passed out and woke up under a sprinkler on somebody's front lawn. They'd carried him off the road. He was incredibly embarrassed after this, only his first training run. He spent the rest of the day recovering at John Reid's place, because Reid wouldn't let him drive home.

John Reid loves telling the story. 'I trained the boys hard and we were a pretty fit group. At the top of Morphett Road is a huge hill. I ran the course, too. Mark was just in front of me and I can still see him getting the wobbles. The next thing, he was stretched out in the back of a ute. I'll never forget it.'

It was in the kitchen that Mark discovered one of his great shortcomings. Sharing a flat with Mark Aldridge, the two rookie South Adelaide players were away from home for the first time. They would come home from training exhausted and starving.

Mark Aldridge remembers that neither he nor Mark knew how to cook. 'One night we were making mashed potatoes. We peeled the spuds, put them in water and boiled them. Then we mashed them up with butter, but they were so soft and runny, not at all like we had at home. In the end, Skip rang his mother and she told him to go through the routine. Yes, we had boiled them, yes we had added butter, yes we had mashed them. Then she said: "Hang on, you didn't drain the boiling water, did you?" Then we realised what we were doing wrong. Bloody idiots.'

Despite being hailed as a boom country recruit, Mark actually had low expectations of himself. His main priority was establishing himself at the club, initially at Reserves level, and completing his apprenticeship with Mitsubishi. He had settled into a routine, fitting in the commitments of both work and football. South was unfashionable and the team wasn't expected to rise from the bottom of the premiership ladder in 1989.

It was bleak under the spotlights at training as the autumn rains fell on Mark's first season of football in Adelaide. What he hadn't reckoned on, though, was John Reid's commitment to giving his recruits a fair go and helping them to reach their potential.

South Adelaide finished bottom of the ladder in 1988 and lost 26 successive games coming through to the next season. Reid said it was difficult gaining credibility as a team and as individuals. 'Mark stood out because of his grit and grunt and his general approach to training. He was a pleasure to coach because he really did work hard. It was just sort of inbred in him. He went full bore. He had some deficiencies with the use of the ball, but he worked hard on that. I don't think Mark ever overrated his ability. I think he understood from a reasonably early age that he wasn't a gifted player and that to make it, at any level, he would really need to put in extra effort.'

As the pre-season Escort Cup loomed, Mark was selected in the league team and it was a bloody and bruising introduction. He came off the bench early as the ball was rushed out of the South defence. Unopposed, Mark ran for it, only to be flattened by the centre half forward and his opponent running for the ball. He walked off covered in blood and, as eight stitches were inserted in his forehead, he thought of Bob Boston's words.

Mark was happy to get a run, and the injury didn't worry him. The week after, the team played West Adelaide and he suffered another gash that needed five stitches above his eye. A fortnight later, he ran into an elbow and had nine stitches put in above the other eye!

Having survived the pre-season games, Mark was selected in the side for the first game of the home-and-away series against West Torrens at Adelaide Oval. It was his league debut and two telegrams arrived at the South Adelaide Club before the game.

> *Mark, best of luck on your big day and for the rest of the season. We know you will do us proud.*
> Solly players, members and management committee

> *Mark, congratulations and good luck in your first game in the big league.*
> Bob Boston

Despite losing to West Torrens, Mark made an outstanding debut. He felt he had played a serviceable game without doing anything spectacular. In the change rooms after the game, one of the older players, Phil Brooksby, came up to him and told him that he had set a standard for himself. At the club that night, he received an award. The newspapers trumpeted the arrival of a promising player with *The News* reporting: 'South was best served by young Bickley. His desperation and willingness to throw himself at the ball was inspirational and he will make the grade in league company.'

The weeks rolled by without a win for South, but the name Bickley was prominent in voting for the Rookie of the Year award. Finally, South's drought of 26 consecutive losses was broken. They beat Norwood, a traditional powerhouse in the South Australian National Football League, by 18 points. South players and supporters were engulfed in euphoria. Even John Reid's 70-year-old mother threw herself into the celebrations with her son and the players.

The Advertiser reported: 'Mark Bickley, described by Reid as South's hardest worker, was best on ground, not only because of his tenacity, but also the way he made use of the many hard possessions he gained.' *The News* said: 'Bickley was an inspiration with his raw courage and commitment to the cause. Time and time again, Bickley was knocked hard into the turf, only to bounce back up and feature in South's next passage of play.' Mark himself was quoted in *The News* as saying: 'At three quarter time, Reidy said this was our big chance, and to keep attacking – not go on the negative. We were in it as a group and nothing was going to stop us. It was just a fantastic feeling. Unbelievable.' Mark savoured his first taste of victory since Solomontown won the 1988 Grand Final.

South soon came down to earth, but Mark continued to figure in the Rookie of the Year voting. He won the award. In one interview, he described coming to South as his luckiest break. Asked who had been the biggest influence on his football career, he responded instantly that it was his father. Asked his favourite all-time player, his reply was: 'Malcolm Blight.'

John Reid instilled a spirit of endeavour and an enormous work ethic in his players. The club was reputed to train harder than any other in the SANFL. Mark believes Reid's coaching style suited his unyielding style of play. 'We were battlers in the league. Reidy promoted an us-against-them mentality in the South Adelaide Football Club. We were grateful for anything that came our way. We worked hard for it. Some people have great ball skills, or great height or are great marks. My view is that you have to work hard for the things you don't have. At the same time, Reidy always reminded us how lucky we were. Quite often we went to the Adelaide's Children Hospital and we'd talk to kids who were terminally ill, or in the burns unit. That's what I mean. Reidy told us never to take things for granted. His theory is that if you keep chipping away and keep working hard, the rewards will come. It's a good philosophy in football, in work and in life generally.'

In 1990, South Adelaide exerted real influence in the League. They beat Norwood in the elimination final, but were soundly defeated by North Adelaide in the first semi-final. During the year, Mark played his 50th league game, but in his own assessment, it had not been an outstanding year. John Reid called it the second year blues.

4
HIGHS AND LOWS

The birth of the Adelaide Football Club took place in an atmosphere of intense turmoil, emotion and animosity. The focus of unbridled spite and condemnation was Port Adelaide, the State's most decorated football club in terms of league premierships. Throughout its history, Port Adelaide had nurtured a doctrine that it would prevail against all adversity. Port had been successful so often on the football ground that the powers behind the club ultimately began to believe they could do the same off it. Put simply, as the doors began to open for a South Australian team in the AFL, the Port Adelaide hierarchy believed it was the right of their club, above all others, to represent the State in the AFL. The fact that the SANFL had nine other clubs with supporters did not enter the equation in the minds of the Alberton elite. As a result, they embarked on a course of action that led to open scorn from just about everyone, except their own supporters.

The arrival of the Adelaide Football Club had its origins midway through last century with calls for a truly national competition. But it was not until 1981 that the concept gathered momentum, as SANFL directors gathered to formalise a plan to enter a team, proposed as the 'Adelaide Football Club', in the then Victorian Football League. The SANFL directors believed the future of Australian football rested in presenting the top level of competition in as many capital cities as the game – and crowds – would support. However, the 1981 proposal never got off the ground. The progress was slow primarily because the SANFL directors, under the guidance of president Max Basheer, refused to proceed with any initiatives that would adversely affect the local competition and a century of tradition. The AFL, on the other hand, continued to push tenaciously for South Australian representation throughout the 1980s. The SANFL withstood the pressure, claiming the terms and conditions on offer were unsatisfactory. Western Australia relented, entering the West Coast Eagles in 1987, which led to the sudden decimation of its local league. The Brisbane Bears – later the Lions – also entered in 1987 and South Australia was in isolation.

As the pressure continued to mount, clandestine meetings were held among groups acting outside the official stance of the SANFL. Port Adelaide continued its push and then Norwood, steeped in tradition and past glories, claimed its right to compete in the AFL. The situation took a dramatic turn in 1990, when Port Adelaide reportedly made contact with Alan Schwab, the AFL's Executive Commissioner. Preceding this, Port Adelaide had twice participated in a unanimous vote of support for the SANFL to stay out of the AFL until at least 1993. The issue became public through a newspaper scoop, and Port Adelaide's secret dealings were viewed as deceit. The club allegedly stated that it could not divulge its hand while negotiating with the AFL. Anger and bitterness reigned in South Australian football. Within days, the matter was in the courts, threatening the whole structure of the SANFL. Port Adelaide were censored by the court, and their attempts to continue negotiations with the AFL Commission were halted.

On 20 August 1990, the SANFL launched its own bid to join the AFL, still claiming it needed time to implement the plan with minimal effect on the local competition. Port Adelaide's position was that South Australia should not wait, because the domestic competition was already struggling as a result of the pressure of AFL recruiting and marketing, with direct television coverage of AFL matches in South Australia. Ultimately the SANFL succumbed to internal and external pressure and agreed to enter a side in 1991. While the deal was signed, there was still an enormous challenge in creating a new football club and assembling a competitive team within a matter of months. Many doubted it could be done. An interim board was formed, chaired by Max Basheer. Within ten days, the first coach of the Adelaide Crows Football Club was appointed: former Glenelg champion and outstanding State coach Graham Cornes. His assistant was Michael Taylor, a quiet achiever who also commanded huge respect as a veteran of Norwood and Collingwood, playing 13 State games along the way. Taylor had also served as assistant coach to Leigh Matthews at Collingwood. A training squad of likely players was assembled, including veterans such as Tony McGuinness, Mark Mickan, Bruce Lindner and Bruce Abernethy, all back home after accomplished records with AFL clubs, along with local stars including Glenelg's Chris McDermott and David Marshall, West Torrens' Bruce Lindsay and Norwood's Andrew Jarman.

Graham Cornes said at the time, 'For anybody involved in the playing side of the Adelaide Football Club, it is a very exciting season ahead. Underlying that excitement is a very real sense of purpose and responsibility that we have to the people of South Australia. I won't, at this stage, speak publicly about premierships, but there is no doubt [that] on every occasion we take to the field, we will have the best available team. The team will be highly motivated, well disciplined, well prepared, and with the knowledge and belief that if they do everything correctly, they will win.'

* * *

The prospect of playing AFL football filled Mark Bickley with excitement and trepidation. From Solomontown to the Adelaide Football Club in the space of two years was impossible to forecast and forbidding to contemplate. His second year in the SANFL had been tougher than he thought it would be, although his form in the final few games had been encouraging. Off the field, there were huge distractions for the South Adelaide players, with the club in financial difficulty and mounting speculation that it would fold or be forced to merge with another SANFL club. Late in the 1990 season, South had played Glenelg and Mark was assigned to stand Chris McDermott, one of the finest players not to have won a Magarey Medal as the State's best footballer.

Mark recalls the game, 'At the kickouts, I had to lead to the opposite side of the ground to take Chris away from the ball. All day, he was saying, "What are you running out here for? You know the ball is on the other side!" I was a bit sheepish towards him, but at the end of the game I thought I did a reasonable job. As we were walking off the ground, he said "Look, if things do fold at South Adelaide, you're more than welcome to come down and play for Glenelg." I was pretty happy with that because, at the time, the future of South was up in the air and Glenelg was a pretty successful side with a lot of really high-profile players. If I had to go to another club, I would have tried to make it Glenelg. I found out later that Chris had recommended me to Graham Cornes.'

Mark first heard the news on the radio. He had just got into his car when the initial squad of players for the Adelaide Football Club was announced. Names were called alphabetically, and he was one of the first. He was shocked, happy and fearful.

Coach Graham Cornes recalls: 'The emphasis was on developing a strong, running, attacking game with quick direct use of the ball, and a forward line structure that gave players room to move and convert. I believed it was possible for the Crows to be competitive from the word go. In terms of personal qualities of the players, we wanted people who were prepared to have an honest, genuine dip. A player has to work on fitness, pace, strength, skill and psychological strength. Each player is different, but, if you ask me, the most important characteristic a footballer should have, is that every time he goes for the ball he needs to be desperate, and willing to lay everything on the line to win it.'

Cornes saw Mark as '... a really interesting case. He played for South Adelaide, and they were not a threat in the late eighties. If you were on your game, you knew you could beat them, so they didn't have any standout players. We sat down and looked at the squad – Neil Kerley, Bob Hammond and myself. We were very aware that we needed to have representatives from each team, so a few unknowns were added, almost gratuitously. One thing that stuck in my mind was when Glenelg played South Adelaide late in 1990, and South played a scragging type of game that was aimed at dragging us down to their level. Mark was assigned to tag Chris McDermott, who at that stage was arguably the best player in the State. Mark did a good job and Chris was very complimentary about the way this kid had stuck to his task. He was very determined and desperate.'

Cornes and the panel selected some players from South Adelaide for the initial squad, including Nigel Smart – mostly because of his powerful athletic ability – and Peter McIntyre, David Stoeckel and Mac Grummett. They chose the best players available, but they also saw the need for young, gutsy players who could develop within the team. The coach felt that Mark was in that category.

In the days after the announcement of his selection in the training squad, as more and more people congratulated him, Mark began to build defences against possible failure. He had already started to let himself down gently in case things didn't work out. 'I'd decided to say to people, "Look there are 70 guys, and they're only picking 52 for the final squad. If I don't make it, I will at least have had a really good pre-season for South." At the first training sessions, the most noticeable thing was the way players from each club stayed together in the change room. A few weeks earlier we'd been playing against each other and now we were thrown together as the makings of a team. Everyone was nervous. A few of the older guys like McDermott and Jarman, blokes who had played a lot of State footy together, mixed quite well. But there were heaps of kids out there, including me.'

From the outset, Cornes asked the selected players in the squad to write down their aspirations. Mark's pencil-written response was interesting: his goal was to play State football. Representing his State was the most important thing in his mind, perhaps because he did not think he would make the Crows' final list. A year later, following the same request from Cornes, Mark was to write that his immediate personal goal as a Crows player was: 'To establish myself as a senior member of the team and to approach the season with a positive outlook knowing we can beat any team anywhere.' He stated that his ultimate goal was to win an AFL premiership, a huge leap in confidence and a sign that he now had a sense of belonging. Asked how the Crows could achieve team goals, Mark wrote: 'By having a wholehearted belief that we are good enough and that we can do it.' Perhaps the greatest early insight into the essence of the footballer who was to lead the Crows by example in two premiership victories came in his response to Cornes's 1992 question about how the team could improve its preparation and performance. He wrote: 'I think we need to be a bit more aggressive and have a few more players who are prepared to get hurt for their teammates. Once this happens, I think it tends to snowball throughout the whole team, creating a "do anything for my teammates" approach. This undoubtedly brings the team closer together and builds the respect between one player and another.'

It was evident to Cornes that the initial Crows squad was not a physically intimidating group. 'They had to have a belief that they were good enough, fit enough and strong enough,' Cornes said. 'But the fact is that they were not strong enough – many were like boys compared to the guys who played in the AFL. They waded into their weights program, and at that stage we only had a little area in a bar at Footy Park, which was converted into a gym. We had to do it in three shifts and Leon Holme, the weights coach, was fantastic ... We exposed them to physical routines and challenges that they never believed were possible. It was an intense training program – 13 days out of 14 in those early days – and we worked with balls from day one to develop their skills. It was about developing fitness skills and confronting physical challenges.'

Cornes had presented to the Board a profile of the team – the profile that he thought the club should present. It was a team he saw as physically and mentally tough, and was representative of South Australia. 'We could only pick South Australians in that first squad. We were unashamedly South Australian, and we had to develop that patriotic culture, although, as we grew, the club had to embrace all of the other qualities of Australian football.'

Weeks of gruelling training greeted the initial squad of 1991. It was harder than any of the players had experienced, and the test of physical stamina and mental toughness began to take its toll on some. Tempers flared. If a player did not make the grade in fitness or showed signs of cracking under the strain, he would be called to one side by Cornes.

'We'd see the coach call over players and they would not be out for training the next night,' Mark recalls. 'It must have been devastating for them. I was constantly expecting to be called over. At one stage, we had to run 100 metres in 17 seconds, have 43 seconds to recover, then run another 100 metres. We did 110 sprints like that and it was torture, mentally and physically. There were two running tracks, and if you didn't make the grade in times, you were sent to the second track. The blokes there still had to finish the 110 sprints, but it was designed to be an embarrassment for them. I remember one incident. After 50 or 60 sprints on the first track, one particular player started to miss the times and he was sent to the second track with a dozen or so others. At the end of the session, Cornesy called a couple of guys over and told them they were no longer required. This player was one of them. He said to the coach: "You're kidding. You made me run all those sprints, and then tell me I'm not required. You could have told me this morning." He was buggered and he was probably well within his rights to be upset. It just seemed so pointless to make him do it.

'But that was Cornesy's way of thinking. He knew we had to rise above previous standards and he wanted to make things as hard as possible to see who could come through. It was designed to make you bust a boiler, to have the bloke alongside encouraging you, and telling you not to give up. It was about building support and respect for each other. Creating a team. In a lot of ways, it was good because some of the more talented and more heralded players slipped a couple of rungs. There was one session at the Institute of Sport where we had to run 6 or 7 kilometres. Cornesy said, "I want everyone to go really hard, we're going to time the run and we're going to rank everyone to see who's the best and who's the worst." Everyone took off and ran as hard as they could. When we reached the finish line, nobody was around to take the times, which we thought was a bit strange. We were all doubled over, hands on knees. Cornesy turned up and said: "How would you feel if I said that you had to do it again? I bet you'd think that you couldn't do it." Then he looked at us all and said: "Away you go. Do it again."

'I had to thank Peter McIntyre, who was just in front of me on that second run. Towards the end, he slowed down to make sure I finished. We all found out early that Cornesy is a tough bloke mentally, and he wanted to instil that in us. He was very much in control. People used to say that Neil Kerley, as the football manager and one of the State's most acclaimed league coaches, was the strength behind Graham Cornes. After all, Kerls did coach Graham in his younger days, and he did rev us up from time to time. I enjoyed the experience of working with them both. But Kerls knew his place. Cornsey made sure everyone knew their place. He was a good thinker, very concise and an excellent communicator. He was most certainly in charge. It was interesting how things evolved in terms of preparing us for games. Quite often, Graham did allow Kerls to say a few words and there was a lot of yelling and throwing punches in the air. But as players became more experienced and confident, they needed less and less of the yelling. These days, there are far too many things to be thinking about tactically before and during a game and, in my opinion, yelling and screaming at players is not the way to go.'

Physical and mental toughness aside, problems were emerging within the squad, particularly among some of the older and more decorated players. After several months of intensive training for the club's first AFL season, nobody had been offered a contract. Questions were asked about injury at training. Concern was mounting among some players that if they suffered an injury trying to win a place in the Adelaide Crows, only to miss out, would their career be over? Would they be compensated? Were there any assurances? By early December, the squad had to be pruned to 52.

'We had a group of footballers who had spent months training harder than they had ever done in the past without any mention of contracts or what they would be paid if they won a place in the Adelaide Football Club,' Mark said. 'Some of the players knew they could be picked up by other AFL clubs on big money with watertight contracts. A few of them were pretty disgruntled about the whole thing.' In retrospect, Mark felt that the situation put the squad members on a level playing field. He was thrilled to be part of it, but he was constantly looking over his shoulder expecting to be called to the coach and given his marching orders.

More than any other player, it was Chris McDermott who worked on unity within the ranks, particularly in encouraging younger players. He was especially reassuring to Mark, who admitted to being 'shit scared' about his ability at AFL level.

McDermott tried to build up a barrier against doubt. He was a motivator and emerged as the natural leader, as he had been at the Glenelg Football Club and at State level.

Numerous functions were organised for the players to mix socially. Cornes, essentially a non-drinker, was very strict about lifestyle matters, stressing the commitment to being professional athletes. However, he did not object to the players having the odd drink or two in a social setting, even if the players felt uncomfortable in his presence on these occasions. If Cornes had a choice of a social drink for the players, it would be Coke – preferably, he said, from the bottle rather than the tap.

Mark says, 'Graham did come along to our social functions, but he would always leave as things were starting to warm up. That's when Chris McDermott and Tony McGuinness took over, making sure everybody stayed together and enjoyed themselves as a group. That's when we did have a few beers and carry on. But, in a sense, it was all pretty well controlled. Nobody was game at that stage to buck the system.'

A few days before the final list of 52 was to be announced, the club declared that 42 players would be selected from the training squad, along with ten of South Australia's most talented youngsters. These were the young players who had attracted the interest of AFL recruiting scouts. This caused further discontent among the Adelaide Football Club squad. They had trained together for months and, as one said, 'We busted our guts out and our positions were in threat from kids who had not set foot on the track.' Among those raw recruits was schoolboy Ben Hart, brought to training by his father because he was too young to drive, and Shaun Rehn, a 'string bean' with great potential from a small west coast fishing and farming town.

At that stage, Mark still thought his position was under threat. At a meeting of players, his reaction was: 'Oh shit, this must be it!' Mark describes how someone said, 'Well, this is the official squad.'

'It was a great feeling, but you couldn't say "you beauty" or jump up and down. It was a formal meeting and, beyond anything else, I just felt huge relief that the work hadn't been in vain. I looked around the room at some of the other guys, and I was pleased for them, too. Blokes like Matthew Liptak. Matty and I became very close because we had a pretty good work ethic, but we both lacked a bit of polish. I think we just scraped into the final squad.'

When the team was selected for the Adelaide Football Club's AFL debut against Hawthorn at Football Park on Friday, 22 March 1991, the name Bickley did not appear. He was required to train with the Crows, but he had been dispatched back to South Adelaide to play, much to the pleasure of coach John Reid, but to an atmosphere of ever-increasing doubt. Despite two seasons in the SANFL, Mark did not have a high public profile. Indeed, many of his workmates at Mitsubishi Motors were not aware of the athlete in the blue overalls. In the circumstances, this did not worry the modest electrician from Port Pirie. If he were to fail with the Adelaide Football Club, the fewer people who talked to him about it, the better.

Mark was in the grandstand at Football Park to see the Crows play Hawthorn. Just over 44 900 other people were there, too, in a swirling atmosphere of hope, disbelief, awe and then chanting euphoria as the Crows triumphed by 15 goals. Nobody could have predicted this victory against a side with formidable champions such as Jason Dunstall and Dermott Brereton. Ecstasy and unbridled confidence prevailed in the Adelaide dressing rooms after the game, and outside the hungry media worked frantically on their reports about a new football phenomenon. The club suddenly had to contemplate a rapid adjustment of its expectations in the big league. People asked each other, 'If we can thump Hawthorn by 15 goals, how will we go against other sides? Could we make the finals? Could we win the flag?'

Of course, these wild expectations were soon dampened. Bruising reality hit the following week with a loss to Carlton. Before the match, former Glenelg teammates-cum-adversaries, Crows captain Chris McDermott and Carlton's Stephen Kernahan, shook hands in the middle of Football Park, a cameo scene in a dramatic rollercoaster ride before 43 850 people. Mark was not on the ground, and he was again overlooked for the third game when Adelaide beat Sydney at the SCG. As one of the lower ranking players on the Crows' list, he had to wait in line behind starring rovers Tony McGuinness, Darrell Hart and Eddie Hocking to have any hope of making his AFL debut. He was resigned to a season in no-man's land, training with Adelaide, but playing for South. In the circumstances, he decided to work his way into the best players for South each week to keep his name before the Crows' selectors.

Mark Bickley's football life took a dramatic turn after he received a telephone call on Tuesday, 9 April 1991. Neil Kerley called Mark at home and asked him to come to training early the next day. When he arrived at Football Park, there was a contract waiting to be signed.

He thought, Bloody hell, this can only mean one thing. If they want me to sign a contract, they want me to play! 'The club told me a signature was essential because I was to be in the side to play Essendon at Windy Hill the following Saturday. I was sworn to secrecy because the selectors had not met to officially name the side. I just floated out of the office at Footy Park. There was no contract negotiation. It was a case of "You're playing this week, so sign here. By the way, there is no base salary, but you'll get $1000 for each game you play."' At the time, Mark was earning $125 for each game with South Adelaide. The pen had little time to tremble in his hand. When the news broke of his selection in the Crows team to play Essendon, there were great celebrations at the Solomontown Football Club. Port Pirie needed a lift and it had come to them from the kid they knew as Skippy.

Mark's AFL debut provided a fascinating insight into the characters of the coaches of the two sides – Kevin Sheedy, the master tactician, and Graham Cornes, the stickler for detail and preparation.

On the flight to Melbourne, Mark was a bundle of nerves. He felt excitement at realising a dream, but at the same time he still questioned whether he was good enough. He was genuinely concerned about embarrassing himself and letting his teammates down. It was a blustery day at Windy Hill, and Kevin Sheedy had taken down all the flags from the flagpoles so the Adelaide team could not determine which way the wind was blowing. In the change rooms, they found that all the clothes hooks and lockers were taken, because the reserves team, who shared the room, was still playing. Mark recalls: 'Kerls was irate, demanding to know what was going on. In the end, he just grabbed all of the clothes on the pegs and in the lockers and threw them into a pile in the corner. He said, "There you go, boys, make yourselves at home." It was quite funny and it really broke the ice.'

Kerley was in his element in the change rooms before a game. About 20 minutes before the game started, the reserve players came into the room and they were milling around, having showers and trying to find their clothes, while Cornes was talking tactics with his team.

'Later, we found out that when we first arrived at Windy Hill, Cornesy had gone into the coach's box and found the window was dirty. He immediately sent our team manager, Barry Downes, on a mission to buy some window cleaner. "It's got to be Windex," he told Downes. "Windex doesn't smudge." Every shop Barry went to stocked window cleaner, but no Windex. Finally, he found a shop that sold the stuff, but he couldn't find his way back to Windy Hill. When he at last rocked up with the Windex and Chux super wipes, we were only minutes away from the start of the game. It might sound pedantic, but that's how particular Cornesey was in his preparation for a game!'

Mark started on the bench, but before he even ran onto the ground, he discovered how knowledgable and fanatical the Essendon supporters were. He was wearing his tracksuit top, but people were calling out and abusing him, saying things like 'You can't play, Bickley!' People in Adelaide didn't know him particularly, but there he was in the suburbs of Melbourne with a tracksuit covering his guernsey number, and the Essendon diehards knew exactly who he was.

Mark came off the bench early in the game. Incredibly, the player he replaced was the Crows footballer he admired the most – captain Chris McDermott. In his AFL debut, Mark accumulated 16 possessions on the half back line and was named among the best players. After the game, Cornes told him, 'The first one is always a good one . . . but the hard work now begins.' Mark's career had been launched – a career in which he was never dropped from the side, except when he was injured.

Cornes recalls how Chris McDermott championed Mark's cause. 'The match committee always stirred Chris that Mark must be mowing his lawns for free, and Mark never let him down. I just loved the way he trained and played . . . he just laid it all on the line.'

As the 1991 season progressed, Mark increasingly respected Graham Cornes for his abilities as a coach and a communicator.

'His preparation was faultless,' Mark says. 'Cornesy would present dossiers to us before every game with a couple of paragraphs on every opposition player, noting whether or not he had a sore spot, and how he kicked and handballed. Our team meetings were really thorough and would last for a long time. Some of the players weren't happy with the amount of detail the coach would go into, but in my opinion his preparation and communication was outstanding. Before each game, he certainly let you know what his expectations were.

'Every Monday, the coach would distribute a form to each player, outlining how many kicks and handballs he had had, and he would make comments on how each player's opponent had performed. He presented statistics and comments on how a player could improve his game. This gave the players a very clear picture about his expectations at training, and what they could do to improve in games.'

Graham Cornes has no regrets about the amount of player paperwork involved in the early days of the Crows. 'I think it was necessary at that time because we came from nothing,' he says. 'Michael Taylor had come back from Collingwood as assistant coach and I really grilled him about the opposing teams and how they did it in Victoria, and Geoff Southby spied on all the other teams in Melbourne for us. I just felt the players needed as much information as we could give them. Looking back, I think it was a bit too much for some of them. Mark never complained. In fact, he embraced this information and read it line for line. Others, like Danny Hughes, who had come back from Melbourne, just kept complaining about the amount of work. That was a great disappointment to me. Shaun Rehn was only a kid, but he didn't like it either, and Nigel Smart's late father – a wonderful man – even came to see me, concerned that Nigel felt he had to digest pages and pages of information about his opponents before a game.

'We were as close to professional footballers as you could be; we were in a unique and privileged position in South Australia, and I felt we had to earn it. If there was some way of providing players with information that would help them, I just felt we should do it. You couldn't possibly interact on a personal basis with 52 guys, and you couldn't sit down with 25 of them one a one-on-one basis from week to week, because there just was not the time to do it. Of course, there were times when I'd have one-on-ones with players, but not everybody, every week … I was at the club full time, but they weren't because most of them also had to work outside of football.'

While happy with Mark's application to what was required, Cornes wanted him do extra work on his disposal of the ball.

'Cornesy also wanted me to get more touches. Initially, I was playing a lot in the back pocket and getting between 10 and 15 touches a game. Cornesy was always saying: "If you could get five more touches a game, you would be a very dangerous player."'

However, Mark was always aware of the enormous competition for places in the side. He remembers that during his first AFL season, there was discussion one Friday night about whether he or Eddie Hocking would be selected in the team. In the end, Eddie was dropped. In that team meeting, Mark recalls Cornes's reasoning. The coach said 'Eddie has all the skills and is a great player, but I just don't think he is applying himself at the moment. If we had to pick the best player, Eddie Hocking would be in the team, but we're picking Mark because he is doing everything he can to maximise what he's got. He's giving his all.' Mark believed he was there through hard work and commitment on the training track and felt lucky that he was doing enough in the games to hold his place.

In its debut year, the Adelaide Football Club finished ninth, winning ten games and losing 12. The club's inability to transfer its sensational Football Park form to interstate grounds was its major drawback. Otherwise, the team could reflect on a respectable season. There were many highlights, including the 'arrival' of Shaun Rehn, and Nigel Smart being selected for the All Australian team. One of the darkest days was 4 May 1991, when the Crows kicked just 4.7 (31) against St Kilda's 24.18 (162) in Melbourne. What few people realised was that the Crows were lucky to have even made it to the game on time. Their flight from Adelaide had been delayed, the bus from the airport was caught in heavy traffic and the driver took a wrong turn. As the bus approached Moorrabin Oval, players were being strapped by the trainers. When they reached the ground, the Crows had only minutes to change and the coach just 30 seconds to 'rev' up the side. After the game, having been walloped by more than 20 goals, the Crows were booed off the ground and showered with warm beer and abuse from the St Kilda crowd.

Mark turned to one of his teammates and asked: 'What would it be like if we'd won?'

Graham Cornes, the first coach of the Adelaide Football Club, deserves every credit for pulling together a highly competitive AFL side against formidable odds. Many, like Mark, could not fault him for his unswerving commitment to substantial and strategic improvements in individuals and collectively to the team. He worked tirelessly to extend horizons, establish new goals and create a harder and smarter football team. Within three years, he was to steer the Adelaide Football Club to its first finals series. However, senior players began to express concerns along the way. Consulted by the club hierarchy, they would ultimately contribute to his downfall.

5
JUGGLING COMMITMENTS

It soon became clear to Mark that trying to hold down a shiftwork job at Mitsubishi while training for and playing AFL football would result in failure at one pursuit, or possibly both. Quite apart from training and playing, the Crows players were greeted with such adulation by adoring fans and glowing sponsors, that pressure mounted to meet everybody's expectations. There were endless demands and requests for special appearances at functions, photographic shoots and media interviews. This began to impose on the team-members' personal time, and it was especially felt by players who had never been comfortable in the public glare. For some, pure shyness was seen as aloofness.

John Reid talks of the 'Hollywood atmosphere' around the Adelaide Football Club. 'Adelaide, as a football city, has a great ability to suck you dry. Everybody wants a piece of the players and in the past some of them have thought perhaps it's a bit like Hollywood. In more recent times, I can refer to Lance Picioane. He came to Adelaide at the end of 1997 and it never quite worked out for the lad. He was drafted by Adelaide as its top pick and played the first four games of 1998. He did not play for the club again, yet the kid had ability. Now he's back home in Melbourne and playing good footy with Hawthorn. I was interested in his comment. He said, "I came to Adelaide as a nobody. I did nothing, and I was a hero." That's one of the weaknesses of the Adelaide football community. But I have to say that the supporters are getting better. They are now more understanding of the fact that players need a bit of space. In the early days, the impact of crowd attention on players was enormous.'

Even in his earliest days with the Crows, Mark was an easy conversationalist, a quality he inherited from his mother. His willingness to meet and talk with people was seized upon by fans and sponsors. He was requested to do things every day of the week and he found it difficult to say no. While Mark felt it was an honour to be asked to attend functions and to talk to others about football, it soon became clear to him that people were laying claim on his time away from his family and friends. It was a pressure-cooker environment for him, in which he was expected to perform as an individual, not just a footballer. In the end, he had to knock back requests for appearances so that he could spend time with the important people in his life. He says that other players felt the same.

While the Mitsubishi bosses were supportive of Mark's football commitments, workplace obligations began to cause problems. If the club travelled interstate on a Friday, he would have to take a day off from work as a holiday rather than unpaid leave. If he was working an afternoon shift, he would take four hours off to attend training and then return to the factory. Instead of relaxing at home after a gruelling session on the training track, he'd be back at work until 12.30 am.

'It was a nightmare, especially pre-season when it was so hot,' he says. 'Sometimes, if training went 15 minutes late, I didn't have time for a shower. I'd just run straight off the park, into my car, and then break every speed record to get back to Mitsubishi by 8.00 pm.

Things went from bad to worse when I had to work nightshift from 12.30 am to 8.00 am. On one occasion, we played in Melbourne on the Sunday and got home about 9 o'clock that night. I'd played a game of footy that day and hadn't had a chance to sleep. Then I had to work through the night. I had to fix some wiring in a distribution board. Nobody was within cooee of me and the next thing I'm fast asleep. It was a crazy situation. As much as I appreciated the preparedness of Mitsubishi in allowing flexibility of working hours, the job was affecting my health and hindering my footy.'

Mark resigned from Mitsubishi and his career as an electrician. He secured a job as a sales representative in the printing industry and later with SA Brewing, providing more flexibility to apply himself to training and playing football. At one stage, Wayne Jackson, the then Chief Executive Officer of SA Brewing – he later held the same position with the AFL – tore a page out of a training manual and gave it to Mark. The heading on the page was 'Leadership'. Jackson scribbled a note on the page that read: 'Some of this might be worth knowing.'

Eventually, the struggle to achieve harmony and fulfilment between the demands of the highest level of Australia's national game and the outstretched arms of his young family left him with no option. To find the right balance between the two most important things in his life, he had to become a professional footballer.

The challenge, of course, was to determine his true value as an AFL player and to persuade the Adelaide Football Club to meet his expectations. In his own words, Mark had been a 'soft touch' in contract negotiations. Having grown up with the game, he was always just happy to play. However, after so willingly signing up for the base payment in his first AFL season, discussions about remuneration from 1992 onwards became decidedly messy. He was aware that some fringe players had been contracted to fend off the approaches of other AFL clubs and that they were offered between

$50 000 and $80 000 a season. Mark played the first season for a base rate of $1000 a game, receiving a total of $9000 after tax. He entered a new round of contract negotiations with more rewarding figures in mind.

'Some people put figures into my head that were probably inflated, and I think I got carried away by it all. I had a manager at the time, a guy who was meant to be reasonably good. But I discovered that if people are supposed to be looking after your interests, you really need to know them well – and they need to know you well. Unfortunately, we did not have that sort of relationship and there were communication breakdowns and stress.

'I was a bit fearful because there was an arrangement in 1992 that no other AFL club could recruit from the SANFL. Adelaide invited 20 or 30 blokes from the SANFL out to train with us, so once again I felt I was training for my future. In my contract negotiations, I was told that some of those SANFL players were quite capable of taking my position in the team. The position was clear . . . sign up for what we offer you, or take your chances. In the end, I signed up for two years. I realised that if I was going to compare what I was getting with what other people were being paid, I'd never be happy.'

While Mark had forgettable experiences with management advice early in his career, he came to realise the need for professional representation as his role and responsibilities within the team became more demanding. He knew it would be vital to have a manager representing his interests in negotiating with the club, not only in financial terms, but in the finer detail of the player contract, which had developed so many variables – from payment per game to a set fee for the year. Then there were the tax considerations.

'These days, the amount of money involved in the game overall is incredible, particularly from television rights. In fact, that aspect astounds me. However, as professionals, and certainly in comparison with other elite sportspeople, I don't think AFL footballers are overpaid. You have to realise that there are some blokes who are just fringe players on a basic rate with their AFL clubs. They may be delisted at the age of 23 or 24 and they've never had a job outside football. People make some major sacrifices to play AFL footy, for example, not pursuing a career path or going to university. On the other hand, there are players who drag thousands of people through the gates and they must be on good money. Good luck to them.'

Mark realised it would be difficult to go to his club saying how much he felt he was worth. He was introduced to Ian Gray while working at SA Brewing. A chartered accountant, Gray was a lifelong friend of Wayne Jackson, before he left to join the AFL. Evidently, Gray had made it known to Jackson that he was keen to help sportspeople who were new to a high-income-earning situation in their sport.

Mark considers the most important aspects of a player–manager relationship are trust and belief that the manager has the player's best interests at heart. In terms of contract negotiations with the Adelaide Football Club, he says he could not have asked for a better advocate.

Mark's contract arrangements in his final years with the Adelaide Football Club reveal a lot about his character. 'In my last three years, I had annual contracts and there are some pretty sound reasons for that. When you are around 30, things can change rapidly. I've never wanted to be a burden on the club. One of the great things about the Adelaide Football Club is that it has provided financial security when a number of other clubs have delayed payments to players or sought to renegotiate contracts. Payment has never been an issue over ten years and that is one of the great certainties that I have had playing for the club.'

6
WALKING ON FIRE

At the elite level, sportsmen and women look way beyond frontiers and deep into themselves to realise their potential.

In the summer of 1992, the Crows prepared for their second season in the AFL. Graham Cornes, a champion footballer, an acclaimed coach, a Vietnam war veteran and a rigid disciplinarian, and Nigel Smart combined to bring about one of the most bizarre and daring incidents in the recent history of the game.

Encouraged by John Reid at South Adelaide, Nigel Smart seized opportunities that sometimes did not come his way easily, and his persistence to succeed took him from SANFL ranks to the Adelaide Football Club. Smart's brother, Jason, had been a major inspiration. Despite having only one arm, Jason played district football for many years, winning numerous awards in both junior and senior ranks. In one of Adelaide Football Club's early Year Books, Smart said: 'Jason inspires me and a lot of other people, because he doesn't know how to stop trying. He's taught me never to give up, no matter how difficult the situation might seem.'

As he had done in 1991, Cornes took the Crows to Rapid Bay, south of Adelaide, to prepare for the season ahead. Rapid Bay is a beautiful indentation on Fleurieu Peninsula, overlooking the waters of Backstairs Passage, which ebb and flow between the mainland and Kangaroo Island. It is a horseshoe bay, flanked by steep cliffs with vast, undulating carpets of grazing country giving way to thick scrub and huge eucalypts, with great strips of bark hanging from the trunks and branches. It is a beautiful part of the South Australian coastline where, on a calm day, seals curl in and out of washpools and schools of salmon drift along the shore. But summon up a southerly buster, and mighty breakers lash the cliffs and boulders. In a winter storm, nothing escapes the grab of the waves and the boil of water in Backstairs Passage.

It was not the spectacular beauty of Rapid Bay that attracted Graham Cornes. Instead, in the burn of summer, he saw it as a place of adversity – a sweating, scratching, tumbling, muscle-melting and brain-sapping endurance ground that would test the character, fitness and leadership qualities of players under his command. For a weekend, the Crows squad lived in a shell of a house, with no power or hot water.

In the army, there in an acronym C3ISR meaning command, control, communications, intelligence, surveillance and reconnaissance. Cornes has always been proud of his army background, and he applied the principles of C3ISR to his coaching, assuming absolute command and control and gaining enormous amounts of information about his own forces and his 'enemy'. Rapid Bay was his pre-season battlefield and a survival course for a group of men who had to draw on more resources than their physical ability to play AFL football.

'Rapid Bay was a direct reflection of my time in the Army when we were constantly tested physically and mentally, and did things that we never thought were possible,' Cornes said. 'It was a fantastic experience for team building and bonding. I wanted the guys to be convinced that there was always going to be something left when they were physically and mentally buggered. Regardless of what was thrown at them ... I wanted them to believe there was something more they could give.'

Mark agreed that Rapid Bay was about teamwork and leadership. 'Chris McDermott, Tony McGuinness and, to a lesser extent, Andrew Jarman stood out as the players who were shaping the team. But there was a huge gulf underneath those blokes,' he says. 'Experienced players such as Danny Hughes and Bruce Lindner had been with us in the first year, but when the squad went to Rapid Bay for the second time they had left the club. At Rapid Bay, we formed teams and set off on a course of 30 or so kilometres. Each team had to take a huge log with them, and every player carried a 15-kilogram roller bearing. We also took with us a stretcher and a 40-kilogram bag of sand. We would run up and down hills and through thick scrub. At any time, one member of the team lay on the stretcher. Having started out at 6.00 am, by lunch time we were physically debilitated. Each team had just eight litres of water to last the whole day. Some of us suffered, while others thrived. I remember a discussion about dropping the 40-kilogram sandbag, but Michael Murphy stepped up and said "No, I'll carry it," and he did it on his own for about three or four kilometres. At that stage, I couldn't even lift it on my own. You started to work out the people who you really wanted to be with when things were tough ... you'd find that some blokes were carrying the sandbag for 30 seconds while others would have it for five minutes. Andrew Jarman's team actually got lost in the bush and they were four or five hours late getting back to the camp. In the end, they just dumped all their stuff and tried to pick their way back through the scrub. They came in at about eight o'clock that night. We'd showered and eaten our tea when Jarman's team came in, scratched to buggery, with blood dripping off their arms and legs. Afterwards, we all sat around and talked about the experience. Some people disintegrated out there in the scrub. There was arguing and one or two even started crying.

'On the other hand, some displayed outstanding leadership qualities, or did the hard things like carrying more than their load, making a bridge to get across a creek bed, or fixing a stretcher. Some sat back and only offered opinions. I certainly recall players such as Rod Jameson, Nigel Smart, David Pitman, Shaun Rehn and Mark Ricciuto getting their hands dirty. Michael Taylor, the assistant coach, was in our team. He was well liked by the players and he did as much work as anybody else. Cornesy, of course, was the general. He had his own water bottle and binoculars, watching the blokes crawl around on their hands and knees.

'But there were lighter moments. I recall reaching a hill and we had to find our way down a rough track. Grantley Fielke thought that instead of carrying one of the roller ball bearings down the hill, he would just roll it. Down it went for about ten metres, then it hit a rock and rolled off on a tangent, finishing at the bottom of a cliff about a kilometre away, in the opposite direction to our course. We gave it up as lost. One 'bomb' we wouldn't have! Then, there's the story about our weightlifting coach, Leon Holme. At one stage, one of the blokes was busting for a shit, so he bared his bum over a stream. Poor Leon was on the other side of a bush splashing water on his face and filling his drink bottle when a flotilla of turds floated past. It was a hilarious moment in a day I'll never forget.'

Later that night, Graham Cornes stood up among his exhausted men and said he was going to introduce somebody who would show them how to walk on hot coals. Nigel Smart had read about the firewalker in an airline magazine and he had suggested that it might be a good idea.

'There was an overwhelming silence,' Mark recalls. 'We couldn't believe that Graham would sanction a firewalk. He did say that nobody would be forced to do it. Eight or ten of the squad – mostly senior players such as Darel Hart, David Marshall and Grantley Fielke – said straight out that they wouldn't participate.'

The willing players jumped into the back of a truck and they rumbled to a quarry where a massive pile of mallee roots had been set on fire by the people running the camp. The firewalking coach, appropriately named David Blackburn, declared that the roots would burn for three hours, after which the players would return, rake them out and go for a walk just before midnight.

As the flames of a huge bonfire licked the night sky, the Crows squad of 1992 were exhausted, bemused and more than a little scared. David Blackburn explained that first they had to control their breathing and visualise walking on something cold, like wet sand or snow. There were about 30 starters, including Graham Cornes. The idea was that they would work in lines of three, with one person in the middle on the coals, and two people either side.

As townspeople and holidaymakers at Rapid Bay prepared to go to bed, a strange chanting noise emerged from the quarry and red embers rose into the darkness. The firewalkers were building themselves into a frenzy, screaming things like 'cool sand, cool sand' and 'soft snow, soft snow'. Those who had decided not to partake, cool heads such as Fielke and Hart, yelled from the sidelines, 'red-hot coals, red-hot coals' and 'burning feet, burning feet'.

'We were in this big shed, chanting and dancing around like idiots, and then some of the guys started throwing rocks on the roof,' Mark said. 'It was an incredible, almost unrealistic scene. This went on for two and a half hours, and then we watched the coals being raked out. The radiant heat was awesome.'

The coals were raked out to the length of a cricket pitch and Mark can remember chants from the non-participants like 'where's the ambulance, where's the ambulance'.

'So we're in this quarry in the dead of night, the coals are glowing and we started to think about why we were there. It was explained that if we could walk on fire, if we really put our minds to it, we could do anything. We then had to form a big circle, holding hands around the fire and chanting: "We can do it! We can do it!" The guys who had pulled out were pissing themselves laughing.'

Since it was all Nigel Smart's idea, he had the dubious honour of going first. Anthony Ingerson held his hand on the right side and Sean Tasker was on the left. Smart took three deep breaths and away he went. Mark describes that moment as unbelievable. 'At the end of the red hot pitch, Nigel just stood in some water and said: "My feet are burning." He was in real pain, and blisters started to appear on the soles of his feet. Suddenly, reality set in and the club doctor, Brian Sando, whisked Nigel away for treatment.'

In the confused afterglow of the incident, shocked club chairman Bob Hammond, who had arrived at Rapid Bay, Cornes and David Blackburn were locked in discussion. Hammond then announced that nobody else would be risked on the coals, but that Blackburn would firewalk to prove it could be done without injury. Blackburn took the three deep breaths and walked across without any ill effects.

By this stage, Mark recalls it was about 2.30 am and the players had no clue as to what had happened to Smart. 'He was our only All Australian, and we'd risked him on a bed of coals. It transpired that the doctor had given him a huge dose of pethidine to ease his pain.'

Channel 7 reporter Max Stevens had been invited to the weekend camp and he couldn't believe his luck. This was a major scoop. After Nigel had been treated, the club wanted to show that he wasn't seriously injured, so they allowed him to be interviewed by Stevens. This was a mistake, because Nigel was drugged to the eyeballs and on national television he appeared saying something like: 'Oh man, I was walking on the coals and burnt the shit out of my feet.'

In fact, Smart had actually been doing well until the last couple of steps, when he lost concentration. His feet then started to burn. In the end, he had a few blisters which were immediately dressed by the club doctor. He was off his feet for two days, then played in the trial game the following Saturday. Mark believes that to an extent, the whole exercise was successful, even though, he says, it was blown out of proportion in the media. 'If it had not happened at the end of such a long and arduous day – if we were fresh and switched on – I'm sure we would have all got through it.'

The incident still puts a smile on Graham Cornes' face. 'Nobody really understood.' Cornes said. 'We had kept it all very hush hush, but because it was a fire ban day, we had to clear it with the Council and tell the people running the camp what we intended to do. They found a quarry where it was going to be safe to light the fire, and then they over-zealously gathered together a big truckload of mallee roots. Normally when you do this, it is just with planks of wood. We went away for a couple of hours to do our psyching up and when we came back there was this enormous mountain of glowing, pulsating red hot coals. It was unbelievable, and then we had to try and rake out a bed of coals, but we couldn't get near the thing. After about half an hour, they managed to rake out a section of the coals. However, by this time our motivation and incentive was shot to pieces. You couldn't stand within a metre of the coals without feeling discomfort.

'We were very concerned. Nigel felt compelled to do it first because it was his idea. I don't think he was ready to do it, but he did. He got some minor blisters so we stopped it. However, I have no doubt that if we had kept it going and all done it, Nigel would have been the only one with slight burns on his feet.'

7
THE MODRA PHENOMENON

Early in his second season with the Crows, Mark's self-doubt began to fade. After being selected in round four of 1991, he had not been dropped from the side, moving from a bench player, to defender and then into the midfield. Having established himself in the team, he noticed significant improvements in his training, driven by greater expectations he placed on himself. Privately, he sat down at the start of 1992 and detailed two objectives: to consolidate his position in the top 20 players for the club, and to play State of Origin football for South Australia.

Many Crows players had represented their State in junior ranks, including the Teal Cup, and also at senior level. As a country footballer, Mark had not been exposed to such opportunities. As a young boy, he had listened to the stories told by older players at Solomontown about the great rivalry between South Australia and Victoria, and how the Croweaters had beaten the Big V at the MCG in the early 1960s. As teenagers, Mark and David had travelled to Adelaide from Port Pirie with their parents to watch champions such as Stephen Kernahan, Craig Bradley and John Platten play for South Australia against Victoria.

Being with the Adelaide Football Club was one thing; being a State footballer was another. Mark plotted his course. He sat down, looked at the draw and committed himself to playing for the State team.

As the season unfolded, his form was outstanding, earning him the reputation of the Crows' 'Mr Fixit'. He was an obvious selection in the State of Origin team set to play Victoria at Football Park in July 1992. The Adelaide media reported '... Bickley is a robust and industrious defender who has subdued some highly fancied AFL opponents. His dash and judgement, his burning zeal and dedication have been acclaimed by the Adelaide Crows.' Any nerves about playing for his State with teammates such as Kernahan, Bradley, Darren Jarman, Tony Hall, Greg Anderson, Mark Naley, Tony Francis, and Wayne Carey – the former North Adelaide junior who was poised for a spectacular career with North Melbourne – were erased within minutes at his first training session.

Describing how he felt at the time, Mark said, 'I think the biggest thing for me was the acceptance. I went out to training, met the other players and shook their hands. I thought that I'd go out there with superstars who wouldn't talk to me, but they immediately treated me as a teammate. Suddenly, I was on the same level with champions and legends of the game.

'Training was awesome. I imagined blokes like Kernahan and Carey might just go through the motions. But they went at it 100 per cent, and so did others like Bradley and Platten ... they were absolutely flat out. It was a real eye-opener for me, because I realised that while these guys were born with natural ability, they also had an enormous work ethic, and this had made them champion footballers. Carey was just a young bloke then, but he was also totally committed to the South Australian side. At that stage of my development, it helped me realise that I had to keep training and working hard to improve.'

The State of Origin game against Victoria was a dramatic, courageous and jubilant affair, and a triumph for Graham Cornes, who remained an unbeaten coach in games against Victoria. Down five points with four minutes to play, Carey kicked a 55-metre goal on the run and South Australia went on to win by 13 points. There were many heroes, among them Mark Bickley, who set up so many scoring opportunities, especially for Kernahan. After the game, Mark embraced the Malcolm Blight Cup and caught the eye of his teammate, Chris McDermott.

Early in the game, the ball bounced down to McDermott, who handballed to Mark under pressure, yet he was able to kick to Kernahan for a goal. Back after the centre bounce, Chris was on the bottom of the pack and he handballed to Mark again. He kicked it long, and Kernahan took another mark for a goal. Mark ran back to the middle feeling pretty happy with himself and waiting for McDermott to tell him how well he was playing. Instead, McDermott came over to Mark, patted him on the bum and said, 'Now get in and get one for yourself.' Mark thought to himself, 'Perhaps he's right, perhaps I should stop running past blokes and go in to get the hard ball myself.'

After being in fifth position early in the season, the Crows limped into ninth place with a nightmare record in matches away from Football Park. In the wild fluctuations of form between home crowds and hostile fans in other places, the Crows struggled for respect. For two years, their away form became almost like a self-fulfilling prophecy. The more the media wrote about it, the more the Crows tried to overcome it, and the more they succumbed.

'The incredible thing was that it gained momentum,' Mark said. 'We tried to put it out of our minds, but it was always there. Of course, there was no real mystery, no great hoodoo about crossing the border. Victorian teams who came to Football Park also struggled to win, but we did have our graveyards in the suburban grounds of Melbourne and at Kardinia Park.'

Mark finished the year in third position behind McDermott and McGuinness in the voting for Club Champion. He was named Best Team Man, and already there was talk of him being a future leader. In fun, his teammates called him the 'coach's pet'.

'It was quite funny because Cornesy had this system of putting a dossier together about the team we were playing each week, and sometimes there would be a spelling mistake or he might have said one guy was a left footer when he was actually a right footer. I was pretty thorough and read the whole document, often finding a mistake or two. The coach, of course, said they were deliberate mistakes. He then started bringing a Mars Bar to training to present to the first guy to find a mistake. I got my fair share of Mars Bars, and that's how the teacher's pet thing came about.'

Graham Cornes clearly remembers Mark's monopoly of the Mars Bars. 'He wanted to improve as a footballer and a person. He did it all without being a pain in the neck. Some people used to tease him about being the coach's pet, but he was still one of the boys.'

Tony Modra was the Crows' first superstar. Idolised, adored, respected, rejected and misunderstood. Modra had come onto the scene in 1992 and through 118 games and 440 goals for the club, his career soared and soured. Along the way, some of his teammates looked upon him with amazement, admiration, contempt and jealousy. Graham Cornes called him a paradox. Malcolm Blight called him unwanted.

Modra's first love was soccer and he had played for the State Under 12 team. It is remarkable that a player who achieved so much with his hands started out in a sport that relied so much on his feet. When Modra's family moved from Adelaide to the town of

Loxton, the kids at the local high school were not interested in soccer, so Modra played football. As his talent blossomed, Modra's brothers, Kym and Rick, both accomplished footballers, urged him to try out for the SANFL. West Adelaide general manager Doug Thomas was quick to get his signature, and he was recruited by the Adelaide Football Club in 1992.

After Modra had played eight games for the Crows in his debut season, captain Chris McDermott was asked his opinion on the high-flying forward as the team prepared for 1993. McDermott described him as a player with enormous ability who 'leads hard, takes a good strong mark, has a nice kick and converts well'. But McDermott wondered whether Modra realised just how good he could be. He felt Modra had to work harder at training and during a game, and he needed to become a lot more desperate for success. It is interesting to note that at that time, McDermott recognised leadership qualities in Bickley, stating, 'Mark is a possible captain of the Crows. He's fearless, hits the ball hard and he's a great team man.'

While Modra disliked training, his ability was undeniable. The Crows match committee was keen to test him against the club's more fancied full forward Scott Hodges, who had come from a highly decorated career with Port Adelaide in the SANFL.

Mark saw Modra as a bit of a free spirit. 'He just didn't understand that we had to run around an oval for three months prior to Christmas, and he wasn't big on stretching or weights. But as soon as the footy came out, he was phenomenal. He just loved to get his hands on it. In 1993, they got him to knuckle down a bit. In the pre-season, he and Scott were neck and neck for the one position, I remember we'd play a trial match and Cornesy would have Scott play full forward in the first half and Mods would take over in the second. Scott would kick five goals by half time, then Mods would do the same in the last two quarters.' The two were almost inseparable in terms of performance, but Hodges had the reputation and he was the favourite. Then, just before the first game in the home-and-away series, he injured his knee and Modra was selected. He kicked ten goals and was named best player in that game.

Thus began a phenomenal career for the spectacular full forward, culminating in 129 goals for the 1993 season, including 13 against Richmond and 10 against North Melbourne at Football Park. That game presented one of the magic moments in the club's history. Modra launched himself over a pack of North Melbourne players and pulled down the mark of the year. The Crows won by two points.

It was the Modra phenomenon that elevated the profile of the Adelaide Football Club onto the national stage, resulting in begrudging respect. But it was not just on the football field that the club was achieving success. Over 462 000 fans swarmed to Football Park for the Crows' ten home games in 1993, including a record 48 522 against Collingwood. The club turned over $11.5 million for the season and posted an amazing profit of $1.12 million. Nothing in the State's history had created so much excitement; not since Bradman had the State been able to boast such a stunning sporting attraction.

'I felt sorry for Scott Hodges,' Mark said. 'He worked his arse off, but he copped injuries, while everything Mods touched turned to gold. It is interesting though because Scott and Mods were good mates. They were alike in many ways.

'There was so much hysteria about our success and Mods was the jewel in the crown. He was just so exciting. Each time he went onto the ground, he achieved things that I'm sure he didn't think were possible, especially his marking. It was awesome. He had a great burst of speed and if you put the ball in front of him he'd mark it for sure.'

It was not just on the field of play that the shooting star from Loxton left people marvelling in his wake. Mark commented that if he ran into anyone from the Riverland they'd tell him Modra was a champion javelin thrower and high jumper. 'He hated having to do weight lifting. But what he lacked in technique with the weights, he made up with raw power.' On the other hand, Mark says, Modra's greatest weakness was cars. He'd regularly arrive at training in a new car – sports cars, including a red Ferrari, four wheel drives, campervans, you name it, he'd have it. He'd buy a car and then sell it again almost immediately. The players used to tell Modra he was losing money, but he insisted he was in front. In fact, car yards had signs on cars saying: 'ALMOST NEW. DRIVEN BY TONY MODRA.'

Graham Cornes described Modra as a prodigious talent. He says he didn't have exquisite skills, but he was close to the level of Gary Ablett with his physical ability and power. He remembers Modra picking up a javelin and throwing it a distance that would almost qualify him for the Australian athletics team.

The rest of the team would be working all summer in the gym, Cornes says, and Tony would walk in, pick up the weights and lift more than they had been striving to attain. He had a natural athletic ability.

Modra was the shooting star of the AFL, but the fame did not sit comfortably with him. Mark recalls everybody 'wanting a piece of him'. He recounts how, when Tony McGuinness came back from Melbourne, he was well respected and considered to be a great player, but Modra eclipsed him in terms of public adulation. Mark remembers going to Melbourne to play Collingwood. As the team's bus pulled up, hundreds of Collingwood supporters were trying to get near Modra. 'Even after the game, when we got belted, they were there again, pushing and shoving for his autograph.'

As much as the club tried to keep a lid on the Modra factor, Mark says there were a few players who were envious of all the attention Modra was receiving. Cornes agreed there was a 'jealousy factor'. Later in his career at the Crows, when Modra was accused of 'misdemeanours', resentment manifested itself into team unrest which was to cause problems for a succession of coaches.

What few people recognised or understood was that Modra was a shy person who struggled to cope with the attention. He was happiest on his own, or surfing the beaches south of Adelaide where the only shrieks of excitement came from the seagulls.

As a member of the team, Mark could see how hard it was for Modra to function. 'Mods couldn't even go to a supermarket without being hassled. He got so big, so fast, and his life was turned on its head. He was constantly bombarded by people and, as a result, he became almost a recluse. If he found a deserted beach somewhere it was like heaven to him, because his personal life was restricted to his house and a close circle of friends. Because nobody knew much about him privately, it just whet their appetites – they wanted to know more about him.'

The pressure intensified in 1994. After kicking 129 goals the previous year – a performance that carried the Crows into their first finals campaign – there was heavy expectation that the magical Number 6 would kick a minimum of five goals every game. In his playing days, Graham Cornes had faced similar adulation. He related well to Modra, but he was a different character. Cornes had always been a charismatic person who was comfortable in a crowd. Yet Tony was a paradox, Cornes said. 'He could be good, then he could be a nightmare.'

Mark recalls that Cornes and Modra were close. 'I'm not sure whether or not Graham saw a bit of himself in Tony Modra, but he really tried to nurture him and see him through the tough times. He provided an ear for Mods to talk about things. The club's general manager, Bill Sanders, also did his best for Mods. I think Bill ended up trying to manage Mods's personal stuff, just so that he could concentrate more on footy. But it got to the stage where he just didn't want to play footy any more. It was hard to believe.'

It was in 1994 that Tony Modra wanted to give away the game that had brought him fame – the fame he resisted. The Modra sideshow impacted badly on the team. Cornes recalls that he was hard work when he let his hair down. 'It wasn't fair on the other guys who did the right thing week in and week out. Tony liked his long lunches and he was easily led.'

Modra was suspended for a game for missing a training session. He had missed training and treatment on the Wednesday night, and had been asked to make up for it on the following night. 'There had been some confusion in Tony's mind about the message and the arrangements,' Cornes recalls. 'He did not turn up on the Thursday night. There was pressure from the match committee and several players to do something about the situation. They were tired of Tony getting away with things like missing training, and I do think there was a jealously factor as well. He was guilty mainly of misdemeanours, but it did call for a serious reaction. The suspension forced him out of the game against the Sydney Swans at Football Park, and we lost. I still feel the decision to suspend Modra was the wrong one.

Mark recalls that the situation did upset a few players, because they were 'busting their guts', training as hard as they could and they couldn't get a game. 'Yet here was a guy who didn't want to play. It was very disruptive. Some fellas thought that if he didn't want to play it was an opportunity to give somebody else a go, while others thought we needed him because he was such a great player.

'I think at one stage, Mods stormed out of Bill Sanders's office and drove away, saying he'd had enough. Then we heard that Mods just wanted to play, but didn't want to train.

'It's interesting looking back at some incidents. We'd have a team meeting and Cornesy would mention something about Polly Farmer or John Nicholls. Mods would nudge somebody and say, "Who's that?" He knew Gary Ablett and Stephen Kernahan, but not too many others. He didn't really know the opposition, or have any historical knowledge of players. He was just a natural who came out and wanted to play footy.'

While he was privately concerned about Modra's attitude in 1994, Mark Bickley became an admirer of the man who clawed himself up his personal slippery dip to play 118 games for the Crows. It was not an easy journey, and there were troubling times under his second AFL coach, Robert Shaw. At one point, he was dispatched back to West Adelaide to regain form and focus. Undoubtedly, Modra was a champion who was unable to achieve what many believe he deserved in his spectacular, if at times moody, service to the Adelaide Football Club. In 1997, he was struck down by a tragic knee injury that forced him out of the Crows' first premiership side. He fought desperately to regain fitness and form in an effort to join his teammates in winning another flag – an effort that was in vain. It was to be another time, and another coach . . . but this time, a coach who ran out of patience.

'After things were sorted out in 1994, Mods realised that he had to train harder and work harder,' Mark said. 'He had his frustrations, but through sheer persistence his form actually turned around.

Mark thought that when Malcolm Blight took over as coach in 1997, he looked forward to the challenge of working with the Crows' flawed genius. Modra had been through a couple of lean years and Malcolm aimed to get the best out of him. They were considered lean years, but Modra, in fact, kicked 75 goals in the 1996 season. People expected him to kick 100 goals every year. Malcolm worked hard with Modra, particularly with his leading and his kicking. 'I think Mods actually enjoyed the attention from a bloke who was a goalkicker and one of the best in the game.'

Modra sustained a serious knee injury in the preliminary final of 1997. This followed a season in which he won the Coleman Medal as the AFL's leading goalkicker (84), and he was selected in the All

Australian team. The injury forced him to miss the winning grand final against St Kilda. Also sidelined through injury were fellow All Australian Mark Ricciuto, Peter Vardy and Matthew Liptak, each of whom had contributed to the Crows success in 1997.

Modra celebrated the premiership with his teammates, but after the rollercoaster ride of the previous five years, there was no doubt that he was enduring personal agony about being struck down on the eve of the most important game of his life.

'Outwardly he was good and joined in the celebrations,' Mark said. 'Mods faced a total knee reconstruction and I thought it would be a real test for him because he had never been happy training. I just wondered whether he would cope with the mundane stuff – the hour upon hour of work with weights and in the pool.'

Modra, in fact, surprised everybody. He worked hard and was diligent in keeping appointments with his doctor. No-one could have asked more of him. 'I'm sure the injury and the rehabilitation helped Mods appreciate the natural ability he had as a footballer,' Mark said, 'and the spotlight was not quite so hot on him for six or eight months.'

Modra drew inspiration from Shaun Rehn, Kym Koster and Simon Tregenza, each of whom had fought back from knee reconstructions. Slowly, he regained fitness and was considered for selection late in the 1998 season as the Crows were preparing to defend their title. But cracks had started to appear in his relationship with Malcom Blight, and there was word of difficulties in contract negotiations with the club.

Mark thinks the troubles began the previous year, when Blight worked intensively with Modra on leading techniques and strategies for holding the ball in the forward lines. Blight wanted him to play in a certain way and for him to prove himself when he came back from injury. Modra played a couple of games without performing spectacularly, then he kicked a bag of goals in the last minor round game against Geelong. Modra felt he was coming back into form, but Mark wasn't so sure that their coach felt the same way. Everything came to a head after the first final against Melbourne, when the Crows lost by ten goals. Modra was soundly beaten in the forward lines.

Blight had emphasised to the team that flexibility was the key. Players should play forward, back or in the mid field. Late in the game, Modra was sent to half back and afterwards Blight was unhappy, criticising quite a few players, including Modra. On the Monday night after the game, it emerged that some changes were to be made to the team. Modra was going to be dropped. Blight and the selectors felt it was in everybody's best interests to let the players know this early in the week.

Malcolm Blight recalls feeling concerned about Modra halfway through 1997. 'Tony was on line to kick 100 goals for the year. Then he went through a really bad patch. At the time, he was talking to the club about extending his contract; he had about 18 months to go. That was not my issue, and neither should it be. But I just sensed that something wasn't right. He used to call into my office every day or every second day, just to talk. Then he stopped doing that. My door was still open, so I don't know what happened.

'In 1998, Tony had come back from the knee injury. He'd played a bit off the bench, and kicked six on a kid against Geelong when we had control of the game. His form wasn't great. In the first qualifying final against Melbourne, we were down 6.6 to 2.2 at quarter time. I thought it was going to be hard to catch them, and I decided to have a look around. I moved Tony up the ground across half back. I did it for two reasons. Firstly, to try to get him into the game and, secondly, to see what his reaction would be. I kept a video of the game, and it wasn't a very pretty piece of tape. I sat down with him on the Monday and showed him the tape. I looked at him and told him: "I don't think you really had a go there. I'm not sure that you really tried. In fact, I know you didn't."'

Blight let him know he was going back to West Adelaide. 'Call it hard, call it tough. Call it what you like. I've been around a long time and can tell when blokes are committed to the cause. I didn't feel he was committed and felt that he should go back to his SANFL club and find some form, just like 15 or 20 other blokes had done in the two years I had been with the Adelaide Football Club.'

Mark recalls Modra's dramatic reaction to his relegation to West Adelaide. 'He stormed straight out of Blighty's office and into the change rooms. He had a big cardboard box and was emptying out his locker. Above the locker was a 100-game plaque and he just ripped it off the wall. Mods didn't play for the club again, and another premiership slipped past him.'

Disenchanted and clearly unwanted by Blight, Tony Modra accepted a deal to play with the Fremantle Dockers. The superstar of the Crows disappeared to the West.

Modra could have stayed in Adelaide. However, Mark believes Modra's decision to continue his AFL career with the Dockers was the right one. 'It was all very unfortunate, but at the time you could not argue about Blighty's decision, because his results were on the board. Looking back though, Tony Modra has been very hard to replace.'

8
A DEFINING YEAR

Mark Bickley reflects upon 1993 as a defining year in the history of the Adelaide Football Club. It was the year of a shocking incident: the sight of Matthew Robran breaking his right leg, after falling awkwardly against Sydney at the SCG. That year also saw the club rise against adversity to clamber its way into the major round for the first time, only to let the chance of playing in a grand final slip from its grasp. Graham Cornes says the club did not dare to believe it could win the flag. The 'haunted' players, who survived from 1993 to compete in the 1997 preliminary final and grand final, did not dare to let it happen again. In 1993, the AFL competition comprised a top six – rather than an eight – team structure for the finals. To make the major round, the Crows had to beat Collingwood in the last minor round game, and Football Park was filled beyond capacity as the home side fought back from a 6.1 to 1.5 deficit at quarter time to win by four goals: 19.21 (135) to 17.9 (111). It was the club's first victory against Collingwood and the enormous crowd was delirious with joy. The game was certainly one of the most memorable in Mark's career.

'At the 28-minute mark in the last quarter, everyone at the ground knew we had won the game and that we were in the finals,' he said. 'Suddenly, a thunderous chant came up around the ground as thousands upon thousands of people yelled, "We're in the finals . . . we're in the finals." It went on for two or three minutes, and I remember thinking, "This is just amazing!" It was almost schoolground stuff, but something I'll never forget. Suddenly, the reality hit us . . . we were playing Hawthorn in the first final, a team of champions including Ayres, Platten and Dunstall.' Mark need not have worried as he was the Crows' best player in that game against the Hawks at the MCG. Adelaide won by 15 points.

In the week leading up to the game, Graham Cornes worked hard at erasing self-doubt among the players. In the second semi-final, the Crows were competitive against Carlton, but they lost by 18 points after kicking poorly for 8.20.

Had they won against Carlton, the Crows would have gone straight into the grand final. However, the underdogs from Adelaide had another chance, provided they could overcome Essendon in the preliminary final. There had been a groundswell of football euphoria in South Australia, and the club carried this momentum into the game against the Bombers. The Crows blitzed them in the first two quarters to lead by seven goals at half-time. Football is a game of centimetres . . . the shaving distance between a goal and a point; the painstaking difference between a fingernail grip on a guernsey and a tearaway run into the forward lines; the desperate leap to pluck a ball from the reach of a pack; the belief that you can extract a little bit extra from your body when your brain says there is nothing left to give; and the inspirational little bit that can lift a team, deflate an opposition and change the course of destiny. But football is also a game of luck.

'A number of significant things happened in that final against Essendon,' Mark recalls. 'Shaun Rehn took one of the biggest marks of the year about 30 metres out from goal. Another goal would have put us eight in front. But Shaun missed it, and I thought this let them off the hook. There seemed to be a sense of relief among the Essendon players because eight goals may have been too much to haul in. After the half-time siren blew, I remember the Essendon captain Mark Thompson going absolutely troppo, grabbing guys by the scruff of the neck and yelling eyeball to eyeball: "Do you blokes realise what's on the end of this?" As we walked off the ground at half-time, I thought he was going crazy . . . in fact, I thought he'd lost the plot. Essendon were known as the Baby Bombers because they had eight or nine guys under 21. But Mark Thompson had been around for a long time and had played in a couple of premierships. He certainly knew what was on the end of it, and he was trying to convey that to the young players. We didn't know what was on the end of it either.

'Cornesy was very calm and concise at half-time and he said that they were going to come out and have a crack at us. Momentum is an amazing thing in footy and they just got some of it going in the third quarter. They were really coming at us when Andrew Jarman got a free kick in the goal square. He was probably the best kick in the side, but he missed from 10 or 15 metres out. I'm certainly not blaming Andrew, but a goal at that stage could have steadied the ship and just made a difference. Who knows?'

Essendon hit the front late in the game and won by 11 points. The following week they destroyed Carlton in the grand final.

Graham Cornes, like many others, has had years to reflect on the Crows game against Essendon, and to analyse how the Adelaide Football Club came so tantalisingly close to its first grand final and a likely win over Carlton. He believes the preliminary final loss had its origins at the beginning of the year.

'There was a serious flaw in our pre-season planning. We only expected to make the final six. We had some encouraging performances in 1991 and 1992. We were always competitive. Yes, we did get hammered on occasions, but who didn't get hammered? In the third year, we just had to make the finals, and we set out to do that. We had beaten the best teams at Football Park, so we needed to maintain that form at home and win a few games in Melbourne. At that stage, our record in Sydney and Brisbane was impeccable. We always knew it was going to come down to the last game of the year against Collingwood, and we came from behind to win. Against Essendon, we played the best football we had ever played in the first half, but deep in our subconscious minds was the thought that we had only expected to make the finals. No one, until then, possibly believed we could win a flag in only our third year. Finishing third, which was a worst-case scenario, was a bonus. But in the Essendon room, there was only one measure of success and that was winning the flag.'

At half time, Cornes felt pretty controlled. 'I told the guys to rest and recover, because it had been a tough month, and to just keep doing what they had done in the first half. In hindsight, I think that if I had really challenged them, angered them and inflamed them, there might have been a different result. But you get what you deserve. Still, it was all part of the building process. It is interesting to consider how much the disaster of 1993 contributed to the triumph of 1997. Those who were strong enough or lucky enough to survive benefited from the experience.'

While the players were shattered about the loss to Essendon, there seems to be evidence that a certain satisfaction infiltrated the collective subconscious of the Crows players on Saturday, 18 September 1993.

'It was embarrassing, but I don't recall it being slit-your-wrist-type stuff,' Mark said. 'I still believe that we didn't actually realise what we had missed and didn't understand how hard it was to get to a grand final. There was almost a feeling that this was only our third year and we'd played in a preliminary final. I certainly believed that we'd play in it again the next year. Over time, the reality did sink in. Now I look back and I'm mortified by the lost opportunity of 1993. Eight or nine of us from 1993 went into the 1997 final series and we weren't going to let it happen again.'

9

DIARY OF DISASTER

Mark's leadership qualities were recognised with his appointment in 1994 as deputy vice-captain, succeeding Andrew Jarman. The appointment followed successive Best Team Man awards. Adelaide Fooball Club general manager Bill Sanders said, 'He is one of several players this club sees as accepting the responsibility of leading the next generation of Crows.'

There were great expectations and an air of confidence at the club. Mark was on a high, expecting the Crows to become a dominant force in the AFL and compete again in the finals. Predicting the ultimate success, he decided to keep a daily diary of events in 1994, believing it would attract the interest of a publisher. 'Steve Waugh had published his diary, and I thought I could do the same thing,' he said.

Mark's optimism was to suffer a cruel blow as the Adelaide Football Club – wracked with injury, dented pride, discontent and a champion goalkicker who just wanted to go surfing – went from one disaster to another, culminating in the downfall of Graham Cornes. There were many things Cornes could control, some he could not, including the increasing number of walking wounded, the blowtorch of the Adelaide media and the rising disappointment of supporters, who represented a major proportion of the South Australian population. There was an uprising.

'With the continued evolution of the Adelaide Football Club, there were triumphs and disasters,' Cornes recalls. 'The triumphs were exaggerated and so were the disasters. It was an enormous emotional up and down. We'd come back from Melbourne after losing games by 10, even 20 goals and a media pack would be waiting. "Why did you do this?" "Why did you do that?" It used to annoy me when the media got it wrong, or when they beat up stories. We didn't have media liaison people at the club then. If journalists rang the club, the calls came straight through to me or Neil Kerley. It was constant, and I guess we were just learning how to do it. You learn to crawl and then to walk, but only after lots of stumbles.'

After an outstanding start to the 1994 season, Mark broke his left foot in a game against Footscray at Football Park. The Crows had lost a bulldozer.

Instead of turning out to be a record of all things wonderful at the Adelaide Football Club, Mark's diary was a downcast document, providing insights into the rising tension and unrest in the camp.

SUNDAY 24 APRIL 1994 (ROUND 5)

Footscray beat us by 17 points. The second quarter was disastrous for me. At the 20-minute mark, I was running flat out trying to tackle someone, and attempted to change direction. My left foot (the one with all my weight on it) just felt like it crumbled. There was also a bone-shattering noise (apt use of words). I knew straight away something serious was wrong. I tried to keep running, hoping perhaps that it may come good, but I knew it wasn't going to. I headed towards the boundary to come off, and by the time I got there I couldn't put my foot to the ground. As the doctor pushed and prodded my foot, I could tell by the look on his face that the prognosis was not going to be good. He suspected that I'd broken a metatarsal – either the 4th or 5th. These are the bones that run through the middle of your foot and join just below your toes. It was a long and quiet ride to the hospital. The X-rays confirmed the break, although it was a little more complicated than first thought . . . The bone was broken in a wishbone shape, which means a screw would need to be inserted.

MONDAY 25 APRIL – ANZAC DAY

Chris McDermott called a meeting of all the players to try to get an opinion on the way we had been playing, and how things were going with the club. It was an open forum with everyone able to have a say at some stage. The points made were noted by Mark Mickan, acting as the club's player liaison officer who, along with Chris McDermott, would take them to the coach.

The main point coming out of the evening was the general lack of enthusiasm and feeling, both in games and on the training track. This was showing in the way we were playing – with no emotion. We weren't putting our bodies on the line for each other. When we needed to dig deep, not enough people were standing up to be counted. The players resolved to be more enthusiastic and show more emotion on the field, such as acknowledging players for little things like tackles and smothers – positive and constructive feedback, not criticism. The meeting was an excellent idea, and it also gave the younger blokes a chance to say what they felt. Hopefully, through this meeting, a new attitude will abound and some minor changes can be made to keep everyone keen and happy.

SUNDAY 22 MAY (ROUND 9)

We got to our seats just as the teams ran on to the ground. There was a huge cheer that made your hair stand up. Over the next three hours, I witnessed what I believe was our worst defeat since we began in the AFL. Hawthorn 22.13 to Adelaide 7.6. I sat with Rod Jameson and Scott Lee in the players' enclosure. We were in a state of shock. We could hardly believe our eyes at the ease with which Hawthorn won it. After our much improved training, and the thought and effort put into our preparation this week, it just didn't seem possible that we could play like we did.

MONDAY 23 MAY

7.00 am training session. Once again, the coach wanted to address the problems at the earliest possible opportunity. Like everyone else, I have an opinion. I think it's not just one thing, but a combination. The first thing is our lack of depth. We have a number of players out of form, but at this stage not enough blokes playing well enough in the local league to take their place. Injuries to experienced players have unsettled the team. The disappointing factor is that none of the 40 to 50 game players, maybe with the exception of Shaun Rehn, have really taken over the responsibility and shown leadership. A good team has leaders all over the ground and unfortunately at the moment we have too few. Probably the most important is attitude. All of the players have shown how good they are, so why aren't they producing? Physically, they are fit and ready, so it must mean something is wrong mentally. Something is holding them back. Copped a bagging in the papers this week.

FRIDAY 27 MAY

There seemed to be a tenseness around the place today, and everyone seemed on edge.

FRIDAY 3 JUNE

The media has been building up tomorrow's game against Collingwood as our acid test, saying we can't win pressure games. I hope the boys can make them eat their words, or I'm sure they will be scathing again next week. I trained alone tonight in the gym, doing various exercises to try to regain mobility and strength in my foot.

SATURDAY 4 JUNE (ROUND 11)

Collingwood knocked us off 13.12 to 8.19. David Pittman joined the already monumental injury list after being carried off on the stretcher with a knee injury. We spent the night catching up with friends over dinner. I wasn't much company as I was too upset over our loss.

SUNDAY 5 JUNE

Jars [Andrew Jarman] is building a new house and they just laid the foundation, so Andrew and Marian decided to have a 'slab party'. It was more of a get-together than a party, with about a dozen of the boys and their partners rocking up and enjoying a few quiet ones and the wonderful BBQ cooking skills of Nigel Smart and Stephen Rowe. It was a fun, relaxing day, which these days are few and far between. With the Crows playing 16 Sunday games this year, the opportunities to have a beer and barbie with friends are pretty scarce.

MONDAY 6 JUNE

Stephen Rowe, Mark Viska, David Pittman and myself headed once again to the gym, where we worked on a set program for 45 minutes using the exercise bikes, rowing machine and versa climber, which is aimed at getting our pulse rates up. Tony Hall and Nigel Smart, both sporting plaster casts on their arms, were put through an arduous running program by fitness coach Trevor Jaques.

We are having another meeting tomorrow night after training.

TUESDAY 7 JUNE

This will be our main training session for the week. Cornsey set the tone of the training session by getting half of the players in red and the other half in blue guernseys. We had to be physical this week, and the coach proceeded to tell the blue team to attack the red team. What followed was an all-in brawl, no punches thrown, of course, just a lot of wrestling and messing around. It was all done in fun, but served as a point that this is how we would be attacking the game on the weekend.

The coach thought it was an opportune time to reassess our goals and talk about the second half of the year.

WEDNESDAY 8 JUNE

As we trained, a steady flow of players with sore spots mingled through to get treatment and prepare as best they could for what could be described as one of the most important games in our short history.

The coach came down to check out the injury list. Graham's wife, Nicole, is expecting a baby on Saturday, and there had been some talk of him not going to Melbourne with us. Jokingly, I asked him about his loyalties and what would happen if the baby did come during or just before the game. Without hesitation, he said he'd be on the first flight back to be with his wife. He explained the two situations: one of a game of sport, the other the birth of a child. He said there really was no choice to make. He also stated that he had every confidence in Michael Taylor's coaching ability, and felt he would be leaving the team in safe hands.

This dilemma may be repeating itself in four or five weeks when Greg Anderson's wife is also due to give birth. I'm sure Graham will be an understanding coach if Greg becomes unavailable.

FRIDAY 10 JUNE

I went to the movies to see *Four Weddings and a Funeral*. It was a good laugh, and also pretty relevant to us at the moment.

SATURDAY 11 JUNE (ROUND 12)

We never got a sniff all day. We were killed by North Melbourne 21.23 to 10.9. They were ferocious in their attack on the ball and we were meek. They had winners all over the ground and we probably only had one, Rod Jameson. The day was a total disaster from the outset. It was hard to comprehend how such an inept performance could come at such an important time.

SUNDAY 12 JUNE

The papers are scathing. Training at 9.00 am at Footy Park. Graham explains that it was not good enough and we watched the third quarter again on video. It showed quite clearly that we just weren't attacking the footy like we know we can.

TUESDAY 14 JUNE

Just when we thought Mods couldn't get any bigger, he defies us again, rolling up to training in a red Ferrari.

SATURDAY 18 JUNE

Attended the seventh birthday of Canteen, an organisation aimed at helping young cancer victims. We met some great people, a lot of whom were suffering from cancer. The outlook some of those people had was just amazing. It really is a humbling experience and makes our everyday problems seem minuscule by comparison.

SUNDAY 19 JUNE (ROUND 13)

Beat Melbourne by five points at Football Park. The coach has given the boys a four-day break, saying he doesn't want to see us all again until Thursday.

MONDAY 20 JUNE

No scheduled training, but 75 per cent of the team went to Footy Park to get things looked at by the medical staff. Mods made the most of his night off by getting away from it all and flying to Brisbane. He'll spend the next couple of days up there soaking up the sun and testing out the surf. Half his luck!

MONDAY 27 JUNE

Drew with St Kilda on Saturday. When we got back to the change rooms tonight, there were about half a dozen boys getting rubs and treatment, including Shaun Rehn, who was sporting the greatest set of sprig marks I'd ever laid eyes on. They started just under his armpit and extended right down to his lower back. It looked like he'd been in a fight with a tiger. The joys of being a ruckman!

SUNDAY 3 JULY (ROUND 15)

Richmond beat us by seven points. The club organised a function after the game so all the players and support staff, along with their partners, could get together and relax. Playing so many Sunday games makes it difficult for everyone to socialise together, especially the guys who aren't regulars in the side. A function like this gives you a chance to have a beer together and get to know everyone a lot better. It creates a club atmosphere, which is what I think is lacking a bit at this stage.

MONDAY 4 JULY

Graham Winter, our sports psychologist, spoke to us at training for about 15 minutes. He made some good points, but probably the best one was that the answer had to come from within. We, the players, must start believing in each other again and try to build up the confidence of the team to the level it was at last year. Most of the boys were pretty buggered by the end of training, remembering we'd only played 24 hours previously. So a few of them were understandably pleased when Graham made tomorrow night's session optional.

WEDNESDAY 6 JULY

After training, Chris McDermott organised a tea for the players, so we could have a chat about the remainder of the year. The first point made was that by no stretch of the imagination were we out of the finals race. The second point was that we had to smarten up soon. The next bit was the hard part, identifying the problems on the field and how to rectify them. It was an open forum and everyone was encouraged to have a say. Most of the comments related to the lack of talk, enthusiasm and team spirit. The next step was to get a commitment from each player that they would do these things at every opportunity on the weekend. I walked out of the meeting with an air of expectancy about the game on the weekend. If we can go over to Melbourne this week and grab the points it will be a special win and hopefully one that will act as a springboard for our finals assault.

One thing that was a bit of a worry tonight was when a couple of players voiced their concerns about the ability of the coach to stimulate them anymore.

SUNDAY 10 JULY

We were thumped by Carlton 20.16 to 10.16.

WEDNESDAY 27 JULY

Training started as usual with the players getting out on the track a bit before five o'clock. It soon became obvious that a lot of yellow guernseys were being worn. The club's policy is that if a player is wearing a yellow guernsey at training, he is carrying an injury and can't go flat out. The coach called us together and said he was very concerned about the fact that nine players were in yellow guernseys. It was the main training session and Cornsey intended to do some competitive work. After discussing it with the selectors, he called off training and said there would be competitive work tomorrow night, on one proviso – that the players wearing yellow guernseys tonight must be fully competitive if they are to be considered for selection.

THURSDAY 28 JULY

Back again. This time, though, not one yellow guernsey.

SUNDAY 31 JULY

Playing Geelong today at Kardinia Park. We headed back to the motel for breakfast, picking up the two main Sunday newspapers. Both had double-page spreads on the so-called doubts surrounding Tony Modra. Talk about bad timing. As if Tony wasn't under enough pressure already, then he has to read about rumours and innuendo about his private life. No matter how much you try to disregard the media and the sensationalism, in the end it can only add to the personal pressure. It is weighing heavily on Tony's shoulders at present. You could murder 10 people and get less publicity. I think the situation is a bit ironic, as the people responsible for putting Tony on such a high pedestal are now trying to knock him off it.

SUNDAY 7 AUGUST

Footscray beat us 17.16 to 4.10 at Western Oval. To make matters worse, I've injured my foot again. This time straining an ankle. Tony Modra's form slump hasn't affected his popularity. Each week in Melbourne he's mobbed by Crows and opposition supporters alike. Today was no exception, it took him about 20 minutes to get from the change room to the bus, a distance of only about 100 metres. And that's with two security guards. To Tony's credit, he is very obliging with the fans.

MONDAY 8 AUGUST

High drama today with a board member calling a crisis meeting, supposedly to talk about the coach's future. As yet, no statement has been made about the outcome of the meeting. There has been plenty of talk around town about team spirit being at an all-time low. I don't think that is the case. We realise we are in this together and we are determined to work our way out of it. There is plenty of joviality around the place, with Jars and Rehnny providing the entertainment tonight. Jars dumped a bucket of ice-cold water over Rehnny while he was having a shower after training. The big fella was not amused and chased Jars around the change room. Jars escaped, but Rehnny has warned him his day will come!

WEDNESDAY 10 AUGUST

For the second time in as many weeks, the coach had to contemplate calling off training due to lack of numbers. There are a few blokes with injuries from the weekend (including me with a rolled ankle), plus five or six with the flu. After a quick head count, the coach finally decided we had enough to commence training. I spoke to the doctor tonight and he said that since I was out of action for a while, he was keen to remove the screw that had been placed in my foot earlier in the season. He said that the sooner I had it removed, the less it would interfere with my preparation for next season.

FRIDAY 12 AUGUST
The club now has a great chance to give its younger brigade some more opportunities and responsibility over the last three weeks of the season.

MONDAY 15 AUGUST
Beat Brisbane by three points at Footy Park. Mods was sprigged on the inner groin area, which, as you can imagine, is very delicate. He was very uncomfortable after the game and can thank his lucky stars the sprigging wasn't another inch to the left. He could have been in real strife.

TUESDAY 16 AUGUST
On the training track the coach gave us his impressions of how the game went. I think everyone knew what he was going to say, although it took Graham a lot longer to say it. He also referred to the bye this week and said not to make plans to go away, as we would be training at 10 am on Sunday and Monday. This was very distressing for Rehnny, Roo, Rocket and myself, as we had all planned to go home for the weekend – Rehnny to the west coast, Roo to Waikerie, Rocket to Lameroo and me to Pirie. The coach explained that our ordinary form started with the last bye when we didn't train. He wants to keep football firmly

implanted in our minds. I'm not sure how my preparation is going to be affected, considering I'm not able to play for the rest of the year because of my ankle problems. But, I'm required to be there.

SATURDAY 20 AUGUST

In Jamestown for a sports night with Pat Mickan (Mark's wife), Andrew Jarman and Brett Chalmers. Andrew Jarman stamped his personality on the night, making it enjoyable for the speakers and the audience. Pat decided that because it was so cold, she would wear her slippers on the drive to Jamestown. The only problem was that she left her dress shoes at home. She made a grand entrance in an elegant dress wearing a set of fluffy white slippers. Have to be back for training in the morning. Coach's instructions.

SUNDAY 21 AUGUST

Rumours that the coach is finished.

THURSDAY 25 AUGUST

The rumours have not seemed to dull the coach's spirit. He's still very much at the helm and demanding perfection, as has been the case from day one. As a player, you start to wonder if they are just rumours. But they seem to be coming from pretty reliable sources.

SATURDAY 3 SEPTEMBER (ROUND 24)

Last game for the season and we got rolled by Hawthorn 9.12 to 6.11. I'm sure a lot of the players felt glad the season was over. Hopefully we can learn from the experiences of this year and come back in a positive frame of mind for the next season. I have no doubt we have the personnel to go all the way. First and foremost though, everybody is looking forward to a break and letting their hair down. Still one important part of the year, though ... our end-of-season party. Six hours and three pubs later, I fell into a taxi. Take me home please. Because of our exhibition game in London, we have to maintain a training regimen so we are in good enough shape to play.

SUNDAY 4 SEPTEMBER
Met up with the boys again at about 8.30 pm. Only the serious drinkers left, led by the captain and vice-captain and up-and-coming stars like Roo, Benny Hart and that great stayer Simon Tregenza.

TUESDAY 6 SEPTEMBER
The Board is meeting with Graham Cornes to discuss the year.

WEDNESDAY 7 SEPTEMBER
Chris McDermott, Tony McGuinness, John Halbert, Michael Taylor and myself meet with the Board.

Received a phone call from Bob Hammond saying the Board had reached a decision and that the coach was to be sacked. It would be announced at a press conference at 2.00 pm.

TUESDAY 13 SEPTEMBER
An air of optimism around training tonight. I think the majority of players believe it is time for a change.

Mark believed some of the senior players – particularly those who had been coached by Cornes for many years – had stopped listening to him. 'Graham talked a lot, and didn't delegate anything. He was in control most of the time, constantly talking to us at training and during the games. Sometimes, you'd heard him so much during the week – at weights and at running and skills work – that you just tended to switch off. If you did that during a game, the message would not get through. Graham had given his all and made an impact. But he had begun to lose a little of his shine with some of the players.'

The Board of the Adelaide Football Club was acutely aware of problems within the team, and it sought the views of a number of players. At the end of the season, the Board conducted a review process where five or six of the senior players, including Mark, were interviewed. The Board wanted their thoughts about the situation and it made its decision armed with that knowledge. It was reported that there had been a player revolt, but Mark feels that was not the case. 'They just asked me my thoughts on Graham's coaching, and I was honest. I said the message was still getting through to me on what he wanted to do, but that his words were falling on deaf ears among a number of players . . . In the end, I think the Board wanted to look for another coach to take the team to a new level.'

The dismissal was a major blow to Cornes, and in some ways he may not have fully recovered from it. Yet there is no bitterness. Instead, he seeks to put the whole situation into perspective, and to explore some positive outcomes. His reflection on this period is philosophical.

'I'm really disappointed that I let it slip away. It is easy now to look back and see where and how it slipped away. We won four out of the first six games, with a win in Brisbane that Bob Hammond said was one of the greatest in the club's history. Then we had a mid-week State of Origin game which we won with the team half-full of Crows players. After the State of Origin match, I think a lot of the team subconsciously relaxed. Then we copped a few injuries, lots of Sunday games which, for players who had to work on Monday, were a huge pain in the neck, no games at the MCG – lots of little things that all added up.

'It became a real grind and a couple of the players became disgruntled and negative. Andrew Jarman's role in the game was being redefined by necessity, and he was resentful of that. The crunch came in the St Kilda game at Waverley when I put Chris McDermott and Tony McGuinness under an enormous amount of pressure about their roles and responsibilities. The relationship between Chris, the captain, and me, the coach, was never the same after that. I lost him and I could never get him back. He had enormous influence on the players, and I think that was the point when I could not contain it any more.

'I'd coached Chris for a long time. He'd been Glenelg captain, State captain and he'd been through the tough times as Crows captain. We had about 10 years of a fantastic relationship, and it was destroyed. Perhaps he had heard too much from me. That had to be a factor.

'It got to the end of the season and my future had not been decided. We were then told we'd be playing an exhibition game in London, and I said we would have to maintain some sort of training program. Chris was so defiant about that. So militant. I just think it had gone too far. I hope that one day we can sit down and work it out.

'When you savage a player during a game, you expect to be able to put things right at the end of the game or by Monday or Tuesday. That is all part of the pressure of AFL football. There might have been some overreaction, but I don't think Chris ever forgave me for my comments to him in that game against St Kilda. It was a crushing time for everybody. If I had my time again, I would deal more severely with disruptive influences in the team, and manage the physical and mental pressures on the team much better. And I think the club would deal with it differently as well. But again, it's just part of the growing process.'

10
WILDERNESS YEARS

Essendon Football Club is elevated commandingly above its surroundings in suburban Melbourne. The ground is known as Windy Hill, for reasons that require little explanation, except to say that Essendon has been cold and unforgiving of opposing teams and supporters that dared to challenge its reputation as a powerhouse of the AFL. Essendon coach Kevin Sheedy nurtures the Bomber tradition with the zeal that old soldiers apply to their battalions. For two decades, he has called the shots with precision, constantly overseeing an evolution of youth, talent and unyielding commitment to the Bomber doctrine. There is no doubt that Essendon owes much of its self-belief and stability to Sheedy. And there is no doubt that the club's success is deeply rooted in the houses, sheds and shop corners that surround Windy Hill. People walk out of their front doors, cross the road and go into the club. Second home, second nature. Kids can kick a screw punt from their front gardens and bounce the footy through the gates of Windy Hill. Within easy reach of the people, the welcome mat is always out.

There are no pretensions or anything flash about the Essendon Football Club. The grandstands are grey and cold, turning to mud-black and red with a crowd. Below them, the players' room and offices of coaches and support staff are functional. This inner sanctum is knee-deep in tradition and rich in the aroma of sweat, boot leather and liniment.

It is in this environment that Robert Shaw feels very much at home, and rightly so. Over eight injury-plagued seasons, the knuckly backman bandaged together 51 league games for the Essendon Football Club. Later, Fitzroy Football Club – rich in its own football ancestry but beleaguered financially – sought Shaw as its coach. Fitzroy did not prosper under his direction over 86 games, but there were times when the club was inspired, unleashing lion-hearted displays that left opponents sore and bewildered.

After Graham Cornes, the Adelaide Football Club sought the influence of an outsider, preferably somebody from the school of hard knocks – somebody who would give glamour a wide berth and lead the Crows with a socks-down approach to football. In Shaw, the club saw an undecorated footballer and coach, but a tough, fundamental and uncompromising character who was right for the time.

'I gave my notice at Fitzroy before the end of the 1994 season, and it was generally perceived at that stage that I had been offered the coaching position at Adelaide,' Shaw said. 'But Bill Sanders had only just approached me.'

Shaw recalls the general perception that the Crows club had probably gone too long with the same group of players and that they were pretty easy to plan against – McDermott, McGuinness and Jarman in the centre and Modra at full forward every week. 'Fitzroy had beaten the Crows a couple of times and I think the way we did it engineered a bit of interest. But I did not chase the job, and I did not think they'd come and look at me. However, things moved pretty quickly after the Cornes announcement.

'I felt very honoured that an interstate side would approach me, and I was impressed with the professionalism of the club management.' Shaw saw the Crows as a very South Australian side, and an ageing side. His brief was to open up the doors and boundaries a little, especially in recruiting and developing the team. It had surprised and interested him that the 1994 Adelaide team was basically the same as the 1993 preliminary final side without an injection of younger players. 'That is what I based my whole approach on when I accepted the position as coach of the Adelaide Football Club. I set out to develop a more vibrant and flexible combination.'

Upon his appointment, Shaw challenged the players to be the most exciting, passionate team in the game. 'Why can't we become the most close-knit team, the best tackling team, the hardest working team,' he asked them. 'This football team has been called soft. That's an insult.'

Shaw's attitude was that most AFL games were won by attrition and the survival of the fittest. In the lead-up to his first season with the Crows, he said: 'All I am interested in are people who are interested in the Adelaide Football Club. Anyone else, or anything else, is totally irrelevant to me – any other person, any other issue, any other organisation. We have 46 000 people who are fully supportive of the Adelaide Football Club and that's what I'm interested in.'

It was a statement aimed at creating unity and common purpose. But the new coach was not 'embraced' by some members of the team and a rampant supporter base that, it can be argued, was still bogged down in parochialism, unwilling to accept an outsider. There is no doubt that Crows supporters are different, demanding and draining. Two coaches – Shaw and Malcolm Blight — will testify to that. Certainly, there were forces against Robert Shaw, and things over which he had no control, including ageing footballers to whom the club was contractually committed. He also walked into a long shadow in terms of injury. In 1994, Shaun Rehn rucked his way to All Australian selection, and was named Club Champion. On April 16 1995 – just three games into the new season – Rehn suffered the first of three shocking knee injuries. Over two seasons, Shaw had access to Rehn's skills and influence for little more than a handful of games, as the Crows' most important player succumbed to another knee injury and reconstruction in early 1996.

Of that time, Shaw says, 'Even my worst enemy would say that if we had Rehn available for every game, we would have had a chance of making the finals both years. But we didn't, and everyone was constantly in a tense frame of mind. It was devastating. However, we did have wonderful service from David Pittman.'

Shaw's first season at the club was a case of walking wounded, including the precociously talented Jonathon Ross, Stephen Rowe, Rodney Maynard, Tony Hall, Matthew Liptak, Anthony Ingerson, Matthew Robran, David Brown and Tony McGuinness. The wheels had fallen off upfield and Tony Modra, himself sidelined with injury for six games, managed only 42 goals in 1995.

Mark, too, was physically encumbered by a foot injury that had kept him sidelined for much of 1994. Having been elevated to the vice-captaincy under Tony McGuinness, he was desperate to be fit to show his best form for the new coach. However, a relapse of the injury during pre-season training left him anguishing about his future. When Mark broke the bone in his left foot against Footscray in April 1994, doctors inserted a stainless steel pin to help the injury heal. After a long and frustrating absence, he made a tentative comeback, only to twist the same ankle in the return bout with Footscray in round 20.

'The doctors told me that as I would not play again for the rest of the season it would be advisable to go into hospital and have the pin taken out of my foot, saying this would give the bone time to mend and I'd be okay for the pre-season. Later, Robert came to the club as the new coach, and we were all pretty impressed with him.

Our view was that 1994 was an aberration and that under a new coach with fresh ideas we would make the finals in 1995. However, in the second to last training session before Christmas, I went to change direction on the oval and felt the bone crunch in my foot. Robert called me over and he wasn't happy. I said, 'Look Robert, I've just broken my foot again.' He was angry that the medical staff had allowed the pin to be taken out in the first place, but he also disturbed me with his comments. He said something like, "... sometimes players don't come back from bad foot injuries. This could be the end of your career unless you get it right."

'I was shattered ... lost for words. There I was, in pain and, at 25 years of age, being told by a new coach that my career might be over. Certainly, he was disappointed because I think he saw me as a key player in his first season with the club. But I thought it was totally inappropriate and irrational to suggest I might not play again. I had to go back into hospital and have another pin inserted in the ankle, leaving me in plaster through January and into February. I missed all the trial games and struggled through the whole of 1995. The pre-season is the foundation and I just didn't have a solid fitness base.

'My form was poor through the year. Guys like McGuinness and McDermott were getting a bit older and feeling the pinch as well. There was no pressure on Robert when he was coaching at Fitzroy because they were the bottom side. They had no facilities and were always up against the odds. But he came to a club seemingly with a lot of potential and, like the rest of us, he felt the heat when things didn't work out.'

The Adelaide Football Club, which was supposed to rise to the Shaw creed, finished the 1995 season in 11th position, with only nine wins. However, history shows that Crows supporters should perhaps be more forgiving of Robert Shaw. In his injury-ridden debut year, the club recruited or drafted individuals who would become some of its most exciting and inspiring players, including

Troy Bond, Peter Caven, Darren Jarman, Kym Koster, Peter Vardy, Tyson Edwards and Kane Johnson. Edwards and a youngster named Andrew McLeod made their AFL debuts, and Mark Ricciuto showed strength and stature beyond his years. Later, Shaw was instrumental in some further intuitive and revelational additions, including Shane Ellen and Simon Goodwin. The irony is that with all of Shaw's foresight about these players and their natural assets, they produced their best under the guidance of another coach.

In 1996, the Crows started in spectacular fashion with four consecutive victories against Sydney, Fitzroy, Geelong and Essendon. But the club, once again stricken with long term injuries to Rehn, Simon Tregenza, Kym Koster and club champion Matt Connell, lost 14 of the next 18 games.

In the end, the personal criticism of Shaw's coaching began to impact on his wife and children and – as a loyal family man – his priority was their happiness. Shaw, now revelling in his involvement as assistant coach at Essendon, reflects on his time with the Crows and the frustrations he encountered. But he speaks with enormous pride about the recruiting efforts during his term as coach.

'There always had to be an injection of youth. That is what I based my whole approach on when I accepted the position as coach of the Adelaide Football Club. I told the club it could not win a premiership with Modra at full forward. I know he was injured in 1996, and he might have played in the club's first premiership team. But the whole team focus was on Modra. He needed to be more flexible and adaptable. I believe in a team culture.

'Regardless of my win–loss ratio, the reason the club got me was to go in without tunnel vision and to look at the big picture. We had to take a broader spectrum on recruiting, and I maintain to this day that I carried out my brief. I am very proud of the enormous amount of work that went into getting the right types of players into that football club to complement the likes of Mark Bickley, Mark Ricciuto, Ben Hart and Shaun Rehn.

Adelaide was never going to win a premiership with the ageing players they had. Someone had to come in and make themselves extremely unpopular. Some of the so-called icons of South Australian football had never been sat down and told, "You're not playing this week because we are playing a 17-year-old." If that made me unpopular, I am very relaxed about it. I did not have the confidence in myself, or the support or encouragement of people to go all the way. The fact that these players were under contract meant that I couldn't do anything about it.

'I knew from day two, three and four that I was going to have problems. I had experienced players coming in and saying things like, "I'm glad you're here." They were bagging Graham Cornes, whom I played State football against. I thought this meant trouble. I never got that from the younger blokes. Looking back on it, the younger blokes must have found it very, very difficult.

'I remember taking all the older players out to dinner. I told them nobody was guaranteed a game and that I was going to give players like Peter Vardy, Tyson Edwards and Matt Connell a go. I wanted to be really honest with them, to say that they had done a fantastic job, but this was the direction the club was heading. I think they left that meeting thinking to themselves, "let's see how he goes about this." I have no regrets about doing it. I'd do it again. At the end of the day, there were a few older players who held the club back.'

Shaw still resents the Adelaide media's treatment of him and the behaviour of people who questioned his judgement.

'The media laughed at me in a humiliating sort of way about Caven. I can remember an article with a headline 'PETER WHO?' I'll tell you who he was ... your centre half back for two premierships. I am proud that I had the guts to stand up against that sort of media and public pressure. The club needed role models and strong characters like Caven, Jason McCartney and Kym Koster. Those types of blokes are not about self-preservation. They know what team football is all about.

'We got players from the Northern Territory and Sydney. We pinched them from Footscray, Collingwood and country Victoria. Andrew McLeod was a great recruiting coup – Bill Sanders worked his backside off for that one. The recruiting was a team effort that involved Bill, James Fantasia, Tim Johnson and myself. Bill would ask my opinion of a player, then he'd engineer things.

'We were always around the mark, but I could not handle the negativity of people after two or three losses. It was different to clubs in Victoria where you just move on. Then it became personal. Four weeks before the end of the 1996 season, I decided I didn't want to do it any more. I was always finding myself in a position between what I knew I needed to do, and what I couldn't do. People might say I got too emotional or down in the dumps. That doesn't worry me. I think in some ways Malcolm Blight inherited from me what I inherited from Graham Cornes . . . a little bit of player discontent, lack of confidence and a perceived lack of direction. The younger players needed the release of pressure and Blighty's touch. I guess a criticism of my approach is that I was placing the pressure I felt on the players. It was not a very relaxed environment in the second half of 1996, but I could not have asked to work with two better people than Bob Hammond and Bill Sanders.

'The pressure was media-driven. I was under an unrelenting microscope, and there was unfair speculation and innuendo. My only chance was to win two games every three weeks and make the finals. I don't mind media pressure, but personalities and agendas came into it and it seeps very much onto your family.

'I look back now and I am proud of my philosophies and willingness to position the club before my own short-term success. I had to wear the can for it, but if people are really honest with themselves, they will say that I put the club before myself.

'I loved coaching the young blokes, but the sad thing is that I never really got to know them. I'm not saying that a coach should be close to the players. But I just don't like to be judged on perceptions. I hope they understand that. I have no regrets. I am proud of carrying out to the letter what I set out to do, and in some ways I did it at my own expense. I didn't want a third year and they didn't want me.'

Mark, who literally got off on the wrong foot with his new coach, believes the pressure on Shaw exposed itself relatively early in his period with the club.

'Lots of things Robert tried to institute were great, including some of the tactics and training techniques. Through his time at the club, things were changing for the better. We moved into a super new facility at Footy Park; John Reid was appointed General Manager – Football Operations; and we'd recruited a lot of new blokes and actively traded to get players from other clubs. This was all positive stuff. But pretty early in the piece, cracks appeared. Some of us could see that Robert was struggling to handle the intense spotlight being placed upon him. I think the public – like the players – thought that we would make a natural progression into the finals in 1995. After Graham Cornes, we'd secured a Victorian coach, and it was almost like signing one of the enemy to make us harder and tougher. But injuries rocked the club and people were not patient with losing performances. Robert started to be put under the pump, and sometimes that pressure bubbled over and came back directly onto the players in a very intense way. Some of the guys didn't handle it very well.

'But, at the same time, we were receiving mixed messages. For example, in one game we were in front early, but we were run over in the last two quarters. Robert was bitterly disappointed and had a fierce go at four or five of the players. He said they weren't fit enough and didn't know how to push themselves. Our next game was against St Kilda, and at our team meeting on the Friday night, Robert went over to one of the blokes he'd had a dip at a week earlier. He said: "Okay, I'm going to put you on Nicky Winmar this week because I think you're the fittest guy in our team." Fellas started to think, "Hang on a minute, he must have forgotten what he said last week." In sport at this level, emotion sometimes spills over and things are said in the heat of the moment that people wish they could retract. But, at times, when Robert got really fired up he said some things that were hard to fathom.

'In 1996, there was mounting pressure on the coach, and it was almost like a snowball effect. Good coaches have a strong belief in how the game should be played. It is cast in stone. When things were not going well, Robert changed the game plan. We'd move from one structure to another, and I think this unsettled the team. The more pressure he was under, the more volatile he became.

'I think Robert offered his resignation after we were beaten by Melbourne in late June. It was our fifth consecutive loss. Towards the end of the season, Robert told the players he wasn't going to seek another year as coach. He wasn't enjoying it. Why would he want to stay around when it was very much publicised that his wife and daughters were copping a lot of flak. That's not an environment you would wish on anybody. I think about my own position these days with my wife and three daughters. They are precious to me, and I wouldn't like to see them under siege by the media or so-called supporters. I can understand the pressures that Robert faced.

'But, family issues aside, perhaps he wasn't comfortable being the figurehead of an organisation that was under such intense scrutiny all the time. I certainly believe at that stage of Robert's coaching career, he wasn't best equipped to handle the Adelaide media. At Fitzroy, Robert had to battle to get media attention. So he went from drought to deluge and didn't handle it well. After Robert left, the club appointed Stephen Trigg as a public relations specialist. It became part of Stephen's job to handle the media and take away that sort of pressure from the coach. Perhaps if somebody like Stephen was appointed earlier, it would have taken a lot of that additional pressure off Robert, and he would have been able to better concentrate on coaching the team.

'There is no doubt that Robert has an enormous appetite for football – a real passion for the game. He knows players and tactics backwards. He studies the game ferociously, and is dedicated to developing younger players. Kevin Sheedy recognised those abilities in making him assistant coach at Essendon. Perhaps it is at that level that Robert feels more comfortable.

'A coach has to have somebody whose judgement they can trust. Sheedy has a true ally in Robert Shaw because he is a very loyal person.'

Shaw has been determined to put on record his account of the appointment of Tony McGuinness as captain of the Adelaide Football Club in 1995, replacing the club's inaugural leader Chris McDermott. It was generally perceived that Shaw wanted McGuinness as captain, which made the coach unpopular among thousands of McDermott fans. Shaw says, 'The club came to me and said McDermott was struggling with injury. The club said: "Should we reward Tony McGuinness with the captaincy?" I agreed and I have to say that Tony McGuinness was fantastic towards me.' While McGuinness had undeniable rights to the captaincy, there were some who questioned the appointment of a player of a similar age to his predecessor at a time when the coach was trying to build the future on the club's bank of younger talent, including the emerging leadership of Mark Bickley.

Shaw admits he had a lot of problems in Adelaide, some brought on by himself, some brought on by older players, but he says Mark Bickley was never a problem. 'He may not have agreed with me at times, but he was loyal. Mark had captaincy written all over him. He set very high standards and people followed. He is one of the most courageous players I've seen. Tough but fair.'

As the gloomy 1996 season evolved, McGuinness succumbed to a chronic knee injury and he missed a string of games. Mark was cast into the role of acting captain at a time when he was struggling for form and confidence. He had aspired to the captaincy, but in different circumstances. The club was under intense pressure from the public and the media with accusations of poor leadership. Reputations were on the line.

'I was trying to find my way as a leader,' says Mark. 'But we weren't enjoying our footy. We struggled with the criticism from the coach and others, and started to doubt ourselves. I felt this way, and I'm sure it particularly affected some of the younger players, like Ben Hart and Mark Ricciuto.

'As acting captain, I felt an obligation to play better. I put a lot of pressure on myself and that made it even harder. I questioned my ability to be a captain and spoke to a couple of people about it, including Stephen Kernahan, who went to Carlton from Adelaide and almost immediately became captain of one of the strongest and most traditional clubs in the competition. 'Sticks' Kernahan just told me to be myself and stop trying to be the best player in the world – to do what comes naturally. Chris McDermott said the same thing and it helped me through the year when there was a lot of uncertainty.'

Late in the season, the turmoil within the club became fully exposed when Andrew Jarman, whose natural showmanship sometimes descended towards tomfoolery, refused to play. Disgruntled at being played off the bench, Jarman's commitment and legendary skills took a very public nosedive. In the week leading up to the game against Geelong at Kardinia Park in round 18, Jarman was informed that he would be dropped from the side because of poor form. Instead, he would play for Norwood in the SANFL. Just prior to the team's departure, however, Jarman was told to make himself available for the trip to Geelong because of an injury suffered by a teammate at training. Incredibly, Jarman refused, saying he was committed to play for Norwood. This, presumably, was Jarman's counterattack against Shaw. But it only created resentment among the Crows players, who felt that one of their teammates had refused to join them in battle. Refusal to play is not in the doctrine of Australian football, just as it is frowned upon to take your bat and ball and go home if displeased with an umpire's decision in cricket.

Interestingly, Shaw said he wanted Jarman to be more flexible, and during his term of coach he says he gave him the opportunity to resurrect his career. Refusal to play is not, in anybody's book, a good career move. Unwittingly, Jarman ensured that he would become unwanted property in the Adelaide Football Club, and certainly by the man who succeeded Shaw as coach.

The agonising 1996 season concluded with the Crows in 12th position, Shaw back in Melbourne and the club desperately hunting the signature of Malcolm Blight. As the dark eclipse passed the Adelaide Football Club, the spectre of the Port Adelaide Football Club rose just a few suburbs away. Port Power was about to enter the fray, at last fulfilling its destiny.

Having once idolised Port Adelaide players, it was also Mark's destiny to oppose them. The Adelaide Football Club had been formed in a period of intense rivalry against Port Adelaide and turmoil within the SANFL. Little of this ill-feeling had subsided among those who accused the Port Adelaide hierachy of football treason when years before it had angled to become the first South Australian club in the AFL. As Port Power gathered its forces, old wounds began to open. But the Adelaide Football Club itself, and especially the players, welcomed the development, even though they would confront a tidal wave of tradition, something they had sought so desperately to create in the brief history of their own club.

'Respect' was the first word that came to Mark's mind when recalling Port's call-up. 'We knew the arrival of Port Adelaide would bring out the best in us. When a footballer pulls on a Port Adelaide guernsey, he is not only playing for that day and for that team. He is also representing all the other great teams that have played before him. It is quite amazing how footballers you would rate with average ability become world-beaters when they get into a Port Adelaide guernsey. They just have this expectation that they're going to be the best of all time. Some very strong characters created and nurtured this spirit and endeavour within the club. Some people suggest it is a tradition built upon an us-against-them attitude, you know, wharfies taking on the rest of the world. But I don't think they were ever downtrodden – working class maybe, but they were people who could rise to the challenge, never willing to let anyone down. You've got to have a self-belief deep inside you that this is the way it is going to be. It just gets instilled in new players. It is a culture that Port people live by and it moves from one generation to the next. It's something that every football club works towards – a group of players who understand the culture and the expectations, who know the correct way of doing things and toe the line. Everything else follows. Naturally, Port Power proved to be more than a formidable opponent.'

11

A CLUB IN TRANSITION

Shaun Rehn once said his greatest fear in football is losing. With every leap and every muscle and sinew, with unyielding determination, he strives to overcome that fear. Rehn, raised on a farm on the west coast of South Australia, was still a skinny teenager when the Adelaide Football Club included him in its junior talent squad of 1991. He had discovered his football potential while boarding at Immanuel College in Adelaide.

West Adelaide made it happen. Despite Arno Bay being in Port Adelaide's country zone, West was first to recognise Rehn's talent, and he played less than 20 league games with the club before the Crows unleashed his raw talent and unswerving ambition. Midway through the fourth quarter of a slogging contest against the Sydney Swans at Football Park on Saturday, 21 July 1991, the 19-year-old rookie leapt from the bench in his debut AFL game. He was only on the field for 10 minutes, but in that short period an air of confidence swept the stadium. It was the first of so many occasions when the team and its supporters rose to his deeds. The 200cm (6ft 7in) ruckman put in sound performances in his next four outings against Essendon, West Coast, Footscray and St Kilda, before a sensational best-on-ground performance against North Melbourne in the last home-and-away match of the season. Adelaide won the game 28.12 to 16.11. Over the next nine seasons, the club's fortunes reflected Rehn's presence and influence. Three times – 1995, 1996 and 1999 – Rehn succumbed to season-ending knee injuries. Three times he made inspired comebacks, more than could be expected of any athlete. Yet only those closest to the deep-thinking and sometimes complex character who embodied such a rejection of failure, knew of his competitive nature and unrelenting will to succeed. In the quiet corners of the gymnasium at Football Park, they watched him – were inspired by him – as he rehabilitated his mind and body from the shocking injuries, all suffered on his home ground and in front of his own gasping fans. Few football supporters could appreciate the bombardment his body took over ten seasons with the Adelaide Football Club. The scars tell of leaps against knees and sprigs, of swinging elbows and of crunching, game-saving marks deep in defence. And few supporters could understand why he ultimately sought to leave the club to which he had given such illustrious service. But Mark, who had been with Rehn from year one of the Adelaide Football Club, who had been his captain for four years, understood perfectly and supported him to the hilt.

Mark's first memory of Rehn was as a lanky kid turning up to training with youngsters such as Ben Hart, Jonathon Ross and Brenton Sanderson. 'One night, we only had about 15 blokes on the track. It was pouring with rain and Cornsey had us doing an around-the-ground exercise, kicking and marking. If you made a mistake, you had to do five or ten push-ups. Rehnny, being a young fella, made a few mistakes. Only problem was that we had so few blokes on the track that every time the ball came back to him, Rehnny was still on his belly doing push-ups. The coach was yelling, "Just stand up Shaun, don't worry about the push-ups."

He'd stand up, but because he was so tired, he'd drop the mark and then go down for more push-ups. It was hilarious.

'But when he developed, it happened quite quickly. He was a bit like Tony Modra in that he'd try something at training – like a blind turn – and the next week he'd do it in a game. He could pick things up quickly. A few times he had a sore right foot, but that didn't stop him, he'd just play the game kicking with his left foot. The reason he matured so quickly was due more to Shaun Rehn than anybody else. He has such a desire to be successful and a willingness to work on his game. His expectation of himself is enormous.

'When he was up and firing, we'd win games. When he was out, injured, the club generally struggled. His influence cannot be overstated. If the ball is bouncing and he's running against the smallest bloke in the opposition team, he expects to be able to win the footy. That is a great attitude. He also demands that his teammates are competitive. His courage in backing into packs has been phenomenal and certainly made the team walk tall when he was out there. Our on-ballers, like Andrew McLeod, Mark Ricciuto, Tyson Edwards and Simon Goodwin, were able to excel when he got first hand to the football.'

The tragedy is that the knee injuries robbed Rehn of years of football, and the club of the league's best ruckman. They probably also changed him as a person.

Few footballers have been through such extended periods of pain and frustration, Mark says. 'None of us can talk learnedly about it, because we don't actually know what it's like to come back from three knee reconstructions. One can only imagine how hard it was for him. After the first injury in 1995 and all the pain and trauma associated with it, Rehnny came back the next year and played for only a month before the knee gave way again with an innocent turn on the boundary line. Our spirits sank with him. Lying on the stretcher as he was being carried off, he knew that he'd done his knee again, and he knew what lay in front of him. It must have been horrendous, not only the pain and the spectre of rehabilitation, but also the prospect of missing out on what you actually play for – the pleasure of competing and winning.'

In early 1997, the Crows had won one game and lost three – the last in a showdown against Port Adelaide. Rehn came back into the team against the Western Bulldogs at Optus Oval. In the first half, he played with a leg guard, but at half-time he hurled it into the corner. It was an all-or-nothing action that certainly signalled his intent to the rest of the team. The Crows won by 50 points, breaking a 13-month drought in Victoria. The following week, Collingwood beat them by a point, but they won the next five games and turned the season around. Rehn improved week after week.

A strategy of 'frustration', masterminded by Malcolm Blight, unleashed Shaun Rehn at just the right time in 1997.

'It was early in the season and I arranged a one-on-one competitive session for Shaun against Ashley Fernee,' recalls Blight. 'Poor Ashley. Shaun had some real anger in his body, and he was so impressive. He just wanted to play. But I know that when a player comes back from a long-term injury, he is always a bit apprehensive. I devised a simple strategy – I just didn't play him. This went on for two or three weeks because he was still a bit edgy. It was a strategy to frustrate and anger Shaun so much that he'd forget about his injury. Only then would I know he was ready to play.'

Without its champion ruckman, it is unlikely the Adelaide Football Club would have won premierships in 1997 and 1998. He was among the best players in the triumphs against St Kilda and North Melbourne. His outstanding performances in ruck sparked the awesome achievements of Andrew McLeod, who won successive Norm Smith Medals for best-on-ground performances in grand finals. McLeod, to whom Rehn so often fed the ball, won the Club Champion Award in 1998, and he was a member of the AFL Team of the Year.

In the Ansett Cup pre-season competition in 1999, tragedy struck again when Rehn slipped at a centre bounce, shattering his left knee. Mark recalls his teammate's anguish and how he attempted to cope with yet another cruel blow.

'There were certainly some demons that needed to be exorcised straight after that injury. Shaun had to work out his future, whether it was worth all the effort to come back again. I think he may have gone home to Arno Bay for a while. He just wanted to be left alone with his wife, Kerry, to work it out. A lot of things had to be considered, including their young son, Thomas. Shaun would have been asking himself whether he'd be able to run and kick the footy with his son. Then, of course, there was overwhelming public support with well-intentioned people wishing him a speedy recovery. But, in reality, all this did was serve as a constant reminder of injury. This really started to build pressure on Shaun, and it reached a head at the end of 2000.'

In August 2000, at the end of the season, Shaun Rehn – premiership player in 1997 and 1998, Club Champion in 1994, and twice All Australian – purposefully read a short statement to a bewildered media contingent. That was his style, and it evoked anger and resentment from many who had idolised him.

Having read his statement, he stood and walked out, leaving a room and a State full of speculation and suspicion. In time, it was announced that he would join Hawthorn Football Club in 2001. Nobody could really fathom his motives. *Advertiser* football writer Michelangelo Rucci later posed the question: 'Was his mood soured by a pre-season edict from Ayres to wash the cars of two teammates after turning up late for training?' Rehn reportedly replied: 'You don't leave a footy club because you wash a car.'

When further questioned about his emotions at the time of his departure from the Crows, Rehn stated the move to Hawthorn was to revive his career, to find a new challenge in a new environment. He had made a pact with himself to finish his football career without any regrets. And in responding to further questioning, he simply added: 'No one is qualified to stand in my shoes.' It was a typical turn of phrase from a man known for his economy of words – a man who would sooner talk to himself than the media.

Mark's view of the situation is very insightful. 'Some fundamental things occurred. Apart from successfully going through another long period of rehabilitation, Gary Ayres had come in as the new coach and he had a slightly different perspective on the role Shaun should play. Malcolm Blight was quite comfortable with Shaun rucking 90 per cent of the game, and dropping back into defence. But I think Gary wanted him to ruck and then run forward as an attacking, mobile, big man. Shaun was struggling with this definition of his game. He was just starting to get his jumping and timing right when there was a clash of heads in the game against St Kilda, and he finished up with a depressed fracture of the cheekbone. This put him out for a month and sometimes it can be a psychological challenge to come back after having your face broken. He felt under siege all year. He didn't enjoy his footy and I think the constant advice from well-meaning people started to get the better of him. People were saying things like, "It's great to see you back," "You're the best," and "You're great." No matter what he did, or how well he played, people were always going to say, "Rehnny, you're a champion."

'Shaun knew deep down he wasn't playing well and sometimes felt he was being patronised by people around him. He even got to the stage where he didn't want to go to training. He felt like he had lived half his life in the club gymnasium, doing weights and building strength in long periods of rehabilitation. Faced with another year like 2000, I am sure he would have chosen retirement. But, to his credit, Shaun did not take the easy way out. He elected to go to another club that was out of the comfort zone, a club and supporters who would not make any concessions. Paul Salmon and

John Barnes had changed clubs for similar reasons and, I'm sure, Shaun simply wanted to be reinvigorated.

'I would much rather see Shaun Rehn reinvented and playing well for another three, four or five years rather than retiring in regret. People often misunderstood Shaun, and a lot of this was because of his reluctance to talk to the media. That is his prerogative. I don't begrudge Shaun anything, and I hope he goes on to great personal success at Hawthorn. He is a pretty complex, and sometimes moody, type. But he is also an incredibly funny bloke and I have enjoyed his company. When footy is finished for Mark Bickley and Shaun Rehn, I think we will still be really good mates.'

While providing unbridled testimony to the contribution of Shaun Rehn, Mark also reserves enormous praise for David Pittman, the ruckman once described by Malcolm Blight as 'pathetic.'

Mark says that it is important to put into perspective the achievements of David Pittman, who stood up to the challenge when the Crows' top ruckman was absent for long periods. 'Pitto was pretty much in the shadow of Rehnny before he broke down, but when he was given the opportunity, he excelled. He became the club's number-one ruckman, and one of our best performers. He also realised that when Rehnny returned from injury, he needed to have the flexibility to play as a key forward or defender. He worked on that so that he could become an integral part of the team.

'The punishment suffered by ruckmen is amazing, as is their resilience. Every Monday morning, we'd see them covered with sprig marks and scratches. After every game, Rehnny would have bags of ice on his thigh muscles because of knocks from opposing ruckmen, who used to cannon into him. Being a ruckman is the most thankless and punishing job on the footy field. Pitto and Rehnny used to wear metal shin guards. At the end of the game, they'd pull these things out of their socks and it looked like somebody had been at them with a bloody great hammer. Pitto was criticised a fair bit for being injured or bemoaning his lot in life, but the truth is he shared a courageous role with Rehnny. They did it tough.'

After the Crows lost to Richmond in the second round at the MCG in 1997, Blight stated to the media that David Pittman's rucking effort was pathetic. It was an amazing outburst, that brought a wave of public sympathy towards Pittman, and crashing condemnation of the coach.

'There is more to this story than most people know,' Mark says. 'Pitto hurt his calf in the first or second bounce, but he didn't want to come off. Unable to jump or run properly, he was made to look a bit ordinary by his Richmond opponent. At quarter time, he copped it from the coach. After being in a winning position halfway though the last quarter, we had a bad umpiring decision that resulted in a goal to Richmond. They went on to beat us by 28 points. Malcolm thought we dropped our heads. He had a big crack at everyone after the game, and made it clear that it wasn't good enough to get blown out of the water in the last ten minutes. He did an impromptu television interview with Neil Kerley and made the statement about Pitto's ruck effort. By the time we got back to Adelaide it was a huge story. To Pitto's credit, he went to Malcolm and said, "If that's what you really mean, if I'm the most pathetic ruckman you've ever seen, it's no good me being on your list." Malcolm explained his comments and they put the incident behind them.'

Blight's recollection is clear. 'Neil Kerley interviewed me as I was coming off the ground. I was fuming, and I said it was a pathetic quarter of football. We had a lot of injuries and David had to stand up. I was talking about a particular quarter of football, a specific moment in time. In the press conference after the game, I used the word 'pathetic' again, but inadvertently left out the word 'quarter'. I was just continuing on from what I had said to Neil Kerley immediately after the game. On the Monday, I spoke to David because I felt for him a fair bit. By that time, I had read the full transcript of the interview. Because I had left out the word quarter, the pathetic comment was seen as a reflection on David's football career, and I thought that what I had said was unfair. How could I judge David on his previous hundred games? I wasn't at the club then. The whole thing has become folklore now, and I don't think David should be remembered for that. He was a player I never dropped. He was important in the mix of ruckman, tall defender or occasional forward. In fact, when he retired, I thought he was a big loss for the club. He wouldn't be replaced overnight.'

12

INJURY AND COURAGE

While he is happy to talk about the valour and dedication of players overcoming injury, Mark is quite modest about the pain he often carried onto the football ground, and through his own front door. Copping hard knocks and playing with tears in his eyes is something he learnt as a kid in Port Pirie, which is not renowned as fertile ground for shrinking violets. As an AFL footballer, he gained inspiration from the ability of Chris McDermott to play with injuries. McDermott was a warhorse who had played 265 games for Glenelg and nine for South Australia before becoming the first and natural choice as captain of the Adelaide Football Club.

'I don't think Chris McDermott was ever 100 per cent fit when he played,' Mark says. 'He carried a lot of injuries, particularly to the knees and ribs. He trained hard and took that approach into games. He wasn't spectacularly fast, and he didn't have outstanding natural attributes, but when the ball was in front of him and it had to be won, or if a player had to be tackled, he was iron-willed. He was just super-competitive.'

Mark also found Matthew Liptak inspiring. 'As younger blokes, we were both battlers in terms of football skills, and Matt had a terrible run with injuries. He copped a lot of flak from supporters and ridicule in the media. But to come through all of that and win the club's Best and Fairest in 1996 was a great achievement. I have the highest regard for Matthew Liptak as a player and a person.'

It was in 1996 that Mark's courage left his coach and teammates awestruck. In many ways, Mark also discovered he had no limits in his commitment to the team. It was, in essence, an event, an attitude, a resilience, a sheer eye-to-eye contact with the future that assured, with absolute certainty, his ascendancy to the captaincy.

Two weeks earlier, he had played his 100th game for the Crows. On Saturday 4 May, Adelaide played Collingwood at Victoria Park. In a desperate dive for the ball, Mark's head was caught between teammate Andrew Jarman's knee and an opponent. He crashed to the ground semi-conscious, with a frightening 23cm gash exposing his skull. Frantic trainers and medical staff took him off the ground on a stretcher while applying ever-reddening towels to the wound. Mark's recollection of events portrays the drama of the situation.

'Andrew Jarman's knee made contact with the side of my head, just near the cheekbone and the temple, but it actually split open the top of my head. The doctor said it was like splitting a ripe tomato! I remember going down and it really hurt. I felt a warm, gushing sensation, as if I had put my head under a tap in the middle of summer. I knew it was pretty serious because I heard somebody say to keep the towel on my head to stem the bleeding. When I got to the change rooms, our club doctor, Brian Sando, took the towel off my head and dropped it on the ground. It sounded like a beach towel that had been dipped in a bath. Brian Sando actually asked a football photographer to take some pictures of the injury because he had a couple of lectures coming up, and he wanted to show his students photographs of a severe gash to the head!

'At this stage, I wasn't in any pain, but I was in a bit of shock. Brian had to cut off some of my hair to start stitching. I expected to be stitched up and go back out to play after half-time. Brian started stitching and the light was very poor. All we had was a desklamp held by one of the trainers. To make matters worse, Brian was using black sutures – the same colour as my hair – so the job was slow. After every couple of stitches, he'd give me another injection to numb the pain. But I could feel the stitches and was actually counting them. There were also some internal stitches because I'd split the membrane around my skull. Brian put five stitches in the internal membrane, then he started on the outer gash. I counted 13 stitches and half-time had come and gone. I said to Brian, "Gee, you must be getting close by now because I reckon you've put 13 or 14 stitches in." His response that he was about halfway shocked me. At one point, he went to the Collingwood doctor to get some more anaesthetic. I could hear massive roars from the crowd outside every time Collingwood kicked a goal, so I knew we were being beaten.

'The game finished and we had three or four stitches to go. By this stage, I was starting to get a bit upset because the shock had set in. The players were back in the dressing room and Robert Shaw gave them a spray. I heard him say, "Do you realise one of your teammates is in there with his bloody brains hanging out? He might be out of action for six months!" One by one, the players started to file in to the little medical room to see if I was all right. I remember Tony McGuinness coming in and asking me if I was OK. I just nodded and, as he walked out, someone else met him at the door and asked how I was. I heard Tony say, "Bloody hell, you should see it!" By this time, I was crying my eyes out in shock because I didn't know what was happening.

'The doctor finished stitching and I found my way to a mirror. I had a gash from the middle of my forehead to the back of my head. It looked like I'd had brain surgery . . . 37 stitches.'

While Mark was being stitched up, John Reid came down from the coach's box to check his condition. He remembers it vividly. 'I don't think I ever left a room so quickly. It was like a big split in a watermelon. It was as bad an injury as I have seen in footy, and I've been around for a long time. I remember looking at him when he was being stitched up and there was a real look of shock on his face.'

On the Monday night at training, John Reid asked Mark whether he thought he would be able to play. 'I told him it was a bit early to say, but not to rule me out. Reidy had a few helmets for me to try, but I didn't think much of that idea because it makes you a target. At training, Robert Shaw described the loss to Collingwood as unacceptable and reminded us of the importance of the next game against Fremantle. He said, "Look, this game is so important, it's bloody great that Mark Bickley has put his hand up and says he'll play, no matter what." I was a bit taken aback, because I hadn't actually said that. I remember getting a sideways glance from Pitto, who was shaking his head. He thought I shouldn't be playing because it was too dangerous. As the week progressed, there were no headaches or ill effects, so I made myself available to play. Most of the stitches were hidden by my hair, but there were six or seven on my forehead, which I had removed just before the game. I played all right and we beat Fremantle easily. During the game I went in for a ball and someone came running in and kneed me in the head. It was Andrew Jarman again and he was pretty upset about it. But I was fine.'

'I was fine.' What an understatement. Mark dominated the centre against Fremantle. Ashley Porter wrote in *The Advertiser*: 'In a game which sparked little reaction from the biased home crowd because the win was so emphatic, Mark Bickley, who suffered a gash to his skull last week, gave the best hip and shoulder you'll ever see, flattening David Muir. It shook the stands and woke up some of the fans.'

Another football writer, Alan Shiell, wrote: 'His decision to play against Fremantle just eight days after being carried from Victoria

Park on a stretcher was heroic enough, but his strong, fearless performance was as awesome as it was inspirational. He played without any protection on his head, which still contained 27 stitches, delivering two of the biggest, bone-jarring bumps seen at Football Park.'

Robert Shaw said: 'When I saw Mark in the rooms at half time in the Collingwood game, I thought we'd lost him for at least a week. His whole head seemed to have opened up. Then he walked into the rooms after training on Monday night and said, "don't leave me out." I said, "Mate, if you're ready to go, you'll be playing." That was the real courageous part, that he was ready to play on the Monday, just two days after such a bad injury. I didn't have to make a speech about his marvellous courage. It wasn't necessary because it was there for everyone to see. The players and I nearly became a little blasé about Mark wanting to play, and then playing. We really just shrugged our shoulders and said: "So what, that's Mark Bickley." It was a measure of the way he's respected that it was, in the wrong sort of way, glossed over. If it had been anyone of less substance, it would have been a huge thing. But it was still inspirational.'

On reflection, John Reid did not believe Mark would play the week after the injury. 'But, the doctor had said to the match committee that he was a chance. It was a big mental thing for Mark to actually play that week, and I have always admired him for it. There aren't too many blokes around in footy like that . . . players who are prepared to put their body on the line week after week. I've seen blokes who are kamikaze about their football, but I don't put Mark in that category. A kamikaze player is not in control, but Mark is in control when he does that hard stuff. He knows what he's doing.'

Malcolm Blight was to succeed Robert Shaw as Adelaide coach in 1997 and discover first-hand the qualities of Mark Bickley. One of the game's most decorated footballers and coaches, Blight is no stranger to playing with injuries. 'Some players can do it, some can't. Some people probably don't know their bodies. Some people know they've got an injury, but figure they can get through it. Others can't, and never the twain shall meet. Mark is a good example of someone who knows his body. He is durable. If he gets an injury, he looks after himself and if he gets a bit sore, he plays through it.'

13

BLIGHT TAKES THE HELM

Malcolm Blight was quite content in Melbourne. Bought from Woodville, his South Australian side, as part of the legendary North Melbourne shopping spree in 1974, Blight became one of the true champions of the game at every level – Magarey and Brownlow medallist, premiership player, and member of the AFL Hall of Fame. South Australians always saw him as an expatriate behind enemy lines, especially as coach of Geelong. Blight, the absolute realist, did not see it that way at all.

He says he had to move away from home to 'grow up'. Melbourne became his hunting ground as a legend of the Victorian Football League, predecessor to the Australian Football League. Melbourne also became home for Blight, his wife, Patsy, and their children. If it wasn't for the influence of two old mates from Blight's Woodville days – Adelaide Football Club General Manager, Bill Sanders, and Football Operations General Manager, John Reid – Blight would never have contemplated returning to Adelaide.

'I think Malcolm, of his own choice, would not have come to coach Adelaide,' Reid says. 'We approached him to do it . . . sort of talked him into doing it. Finally, I think he felt that he could return and put something back into his home State.'

Blight's reflection on the Adelaide Football Club's persuasiveness is similar to that of Reid. 'Initially, I was reluctant to come back to Adelaide. I'd had two years out of the game after Geelong, and said I wouldn't coach again. I'd gone back into the business world, and had a role at Channel 7, which was good. It was generally perceived that Adelaide had been underperforming. At times they were quite brilliant at home, but away, they were struggling. It was a very uneven team. I left Adelaide as a young player, and then returned as a coach. You see, I really enjoy teaching kids to play footy. Whether it is a good way or a bad way, it's my way. So, in the end, I thought I could perhaps help some kids to start their careers. That was the motivation for deciding to coach Adelaide as much as anything else.'

Crows supporters called it the 'return of the Messiah'. Blight, a veteran of living with other people's expectations, ignored the hype. It was not a homecoming. It was not a case of South Australia versus the rest. 'I didn't feel that way one bit,' he said, 'not a skerrick.'

Among Crows players, the news of Blight's appointment was greeted like the burst of spring, a signal that a long winter of despair was over.

'I can only speak for my feelings,' Mark said, 'but I was hoping like crazy that he would come. He had been the senior coach of Geelong for six years and taken them to a couple of grand finals. We'd heard him talk as a commentator on TV, and he really did portray a great knowledge of the game. He was also a bit of a boyhood idol as well. I just thought this was the person we needed. We'd gone through two years of uncertainty.'

Soon after his appointment, Blight invited Reid to his home at Portsea in Victoria. There, the two old mates and football warhorses sat down to analyse the Adelaide Football Club. Reid vividly recalls the occasion. 'Malcolm and I sat down for three days going through the players – who had to stay, who had to go. We didn't plan to go to the top in the first year, or the second. Nobody was more surprised than us.'

Blight recounts the considerations in that meeting at Portsea. 'We went through the team and applied the 'rating out of ten' principle. With blokes playing at their best, we figured the side rated about five out of ten. There were a lot of unknowns in the equation. In reality, we simply said this is the way we are going to train; this is the way we are going to play, and let's see who we can get to slot into the missing links. We decided to have checkpoints along the way.'

Within days of taking office at Football Park, the axe fell on some illustrious careers. Among those to go were Chris McDermott and Tony McGuinness, the club's first two captains, and Andrew Jarman.

Blight says that every case was different. 'I thought McDermott had retired, and if he hadn't, he should have. There was an incident under the previous coach when Jarman didn't turn up for duty, and that left a sour taste in everybody's mouths. The game is not built on that, and the club itself pretty much made the decision about Jarman. Tony McGuinness was probably the hardest. I made the call, and I thought it could open the door for a new player. Wayne Weidemann had announced his own intentions, and I think Greg Anderson had a year left on his contract. But he'd played a lot of footy, and he was spent. Each of them had been fantastic players. The reality is that you can't go on forever.'

There is an aura about Malcolm Blight. When he enters a room, people notice. With him comes a sense of consequence. Clearly, a genetic code made him a champion footballer. But that code alone did not carry him to the Hall of Fame. He is a strict disciplinarian. His football life is dictated by rules, and he demands that others abide by them. Some may say that rules are made for the guidance of the wise and the obedience of fools. Blight prefers it this way: 'If you don't have discipline, you have too many blokes just going their own way. It is important for people to be themselves and to be creative. But there is no doubt that if you let too many people wander off the track, you'll never get anywhere. You'll finish up with a team of individuals. Self-discipline is important. In fact, I usually hand it back to the players. I expect them to take ownership of the discipline. If I am willing to open up my door and say let's do it this way, and you agree to it, you have to take some ownership of it.'

As the Adelaide Football Club prepared to play its first season under Blight, he stated that he had always believed, whether he was at Woodville, Geelong or the Crows, that coaches must have a plan on which the players can base their game; something that can be measured against, and something that helps players to read and predict what their teammates will do during the heat of battle. In essence, Blight's expectation is simply that players will play an efficient game and, most importantly, that they will adhere to the instructions and plans they have been given.

Blight put the players in a room and gave each of them a document entitled 'Adelaide Football Club Aims and Guidelines, Season 1997'. It was a lofty title for what was, in effect, the 'rules according to Blighty'. The eight pages provide a fascinating insight into his views on the game and the keys to success. Typically, it was written in clear, concise language. It was all very easy to remember with no chance of misunderstanding anything. Under the heading, 'Definition of the Game', it says: 'The game is a contest between two teams, the winner being determined by achieving the highest score on the day. Therefore, the aim is to win each contest and then score goals quickly.' Some may say this is stating the obvious. Others will argue that with the tactical jungle in which players compete today, it is a simple reminder that football is a game of fundamentals.

The 'rules according to Blighty' tell players what to do when the team is in control, in neutral situations or when the opposition is in control. Again, it is all fairly routine stuff about long, direct kicks to advantage, short kicks to 'honour a great lead', switching play, knocking on from congested situations, becoming a handball target, chasing honestly, using your voice, and not going to ground, 'unless you take an opponent with you'.

Blight told players to 'exhibit real concentration when kicking for goal – *your practice method* – and to know your kicking length – *the magic spot*. Don't argue with umpires. When under extreme pressure, RELAX. Analyse why you were beaten – it only takes a few seconds (I am not going to be beaten the same way twice).'

He reminded them about the 'little things in football that require no ability'. Some of them no doubt originated from boyhood – at the beginning of his own philosophical journey in football. For example, he says: 'Look the part. Always have gear in A1 condition (jumper in, socks up). Tie your laces on the side of your boots, or it could distort your kick. Develop and visualise positive thoughts about the game during the week. Sit down and study likely opponents. Analyse strengths and weaknesses. Always be concerned about an opponent, not worried about him. Watch diet and regulate sleeping habits. Even before the ball is bounced, use your voice to encourage teammates. The more you do it, the more confident you become in using your voice. A barometer for success is the number of hard things we do in every game.'

Understandably, Blight is protective of his mantra. But it is likely that his laying down of the law would not have varied much from Adelaide to his ill-fated posting to St Kilda, where he found another irresistible challenge in a club of wooden spoons and broken ambitions – ultimately including his own.

Blight says, 'Football is a basic game involving people with different levels of skill. Len Smith, a doyen of coaches, once wrote 'What Is a Game of Football?' on a piece of paper. There have been variations. We all go down our little tracks, and we all have thoughts about certain disciplines. But it all comes back to that one piece of paper written years ago. There is some added 'fizz, whiz and bizz', but it is still basically a game of football.

Occasionally, Blight drives past a ground and watches teams train. They might be kids at a school or a junior footy club, but he can't help himself. 'I just have to stop for ten minutes. We all get sucked in to just letting the boys train, but sometimes you have to analyse exactly what a player is doing. The technique of the game is super-important. By the time you get some of these guys, they've been doing the same things the same way for years, and it's hard to change. But there are some things you can change almost instantly. Kicking is the hardest thing to change, but just about everything else is changeable to varying degrees, and anything that happens on the footy ground is explainable. I hear players refer to something as pure luck or freakish. But when you actually go back and analyse, it's not that freakish. Things are actually explainable and teachable. Some players pick things up quicker than others. Some have more spring, some have more jump, some have more speed. But there is not one kid who comes out of the womb who can kick a footy. It is all learnt behaviour, so I reckon you can unlearn and relearn.'

Blight strongly believes that footballers should never stop learning. 'What they did last year is not good enough. If you are not learning all the time, you are not excited by it.

'Players play, and that is the most exciting part of the game. As for coaching, if you didn't put somebody in charge it would be a disorganised mess, as it was years ago when the game first started. After being involved in the game for a long time, you see and do many things. In a way, you become a bit of a storyteller. You tell stories of the past to bring players up to what is required in the present.'

In a short period of time, Blight transformed the Adelaide Football Club from one of uncertainty to optimism. He created an environment in which players sought to learn.

Mark remembers sitting next to Mark Ricciuto in an early meeting with the new coach. Blight had told them they weren't allowed to dive on the football, and that they had to stay on their feet at all times. The next rule was that they had to concentrate on tackling players rather than just bumping opponents. 'The previous two years, Roo and I had spent most of the time running around bumping blokes and diving on the footy. It was a strict warning that we had to change the way we played. Blighty told us that if we continued to run around and smash into blokes, our bodies would just succumb to the wear and tear. He told us we had to learn how to run harder than our opponents. This meant being fitter.'

At 28, Mark found he was still learning how to play. 'Some coaches expect you to know how to kick, mark and pick up the ball. They just teach you tactics. Blighty asked certain players who had taught them to kick, mark or handball. Most said it was their dad or the coach at primary school, and he explained that sometimes those people were not experts in the game and, in fact, may not have taught the correct technique.'

Blight took players aside and showed them the correct way to hold the football when they wanted to kick it. He told Ben Hart he was picking the ball up with his feet spread apart. He had Mark Ricciuto practising his take and then worked with Mark Bickley on his kicking technique and helped him overcome his tendency to fall over regularly, something he had done since he was a kid. 'Blighty had the ability to pick up things that were slightly wrong. If we sat down and watched a video of our training, you would almost hope he would find something that could improve your game 5 or 10 per cent. Instead of concern that your game was going to be picked to pieces, you wanted to work with the coach to improve. One of Blighty's many qualities as a coach is that he is a real teacher of the game.'

Tuesday nights were not compulsory for training, unless Blight had found something he particularly wanted a player to work on. Predictably, he told every player they had something to work on in their game, and soon every player was there on Tuesday nights. Mark says the Tuesday night session was more of a relaxing night. For example, Darren Jarman might be teaching some of the players how to kick check-side goals. 'We always liked Tuesday nights because we felt we were doing a bit extra to improve our game.'

The club had appointed Neil Craig as fitness coach, which had an immediate impact. Craig had played many years at senior level in the SANFL and he had worked with the Olympic cycling team under the legendary coach Charlie Walsh. More than anybody else, Craig taught the players how to run, slowly building up their fitness to compete at 100 per cent for entire games.

In the pre-season competition in 1997, Blight's discipline really began to surface. He had adopted a far more serious tone after the first Ansett Cup game. Mark was the first to feel the heat. 'We were beaten by Geelong. On the Monday night, Blighty came armed with a video and he found something wrong with each player, beginning with me. He pointed to footage of me running behind a pack and getting a handball, describing it as a soft way of getting a kick. He then had a crack at every person about something. It was done in a pretty stern fashion, and I think it signalled that it was time to be fair dinkum. Blighty said he would not tolerate certain mistakes that were outside our way of playing the game. He said anyone who moved out of line with the team would be punished pretty severely.'

If a player followed the rules, all well and good. But if he did not, Blight's anger could be of seismic proportions. He demanded conformity in his efforts to change the style of Adelaide's play and, even standing in brooding silence over a player, he was capable of striking fear about the possible repercussions. There was no room for doubt. For example, if a player rushed into the square before the ball was bounced and gave away a free kick, Blight said: 'Don't wait for the runner, just start heading towards the bench, because you're coming straight off.'

Another rule was that if a player won the ball in the centre, it had to exit in line with the Crows' goals. Mark describes how Blight hated it when players went too wide from the pack. He said any player who disposed of the ball over the side line of the square would also come straight off. 'Blighty was also big on the "three strikes and you're out" rule. For example, if you're standing on the left side of your opponent and the ball comes out of the centre to his right side, the coach would say that's his good luck. If you stand in the same spot, and it goes to him again, it would be "shit, that's my bad luck." If it happens again, you know you're coming off. His good luck, your bad luck, and you're out!

'Blighty didn't like us to tag players from the start of a game, either. If the opposing player was having a rotten day, we'd waste one of our players running around on him. Blight would say: "Let's wait until he's had three or four touches, and then consider a tag."'

Blight also had a philosophy about not badmouthing opponents, especially if the team was winning. He would say: 'Why would you badmouth your opponent when it just gives them ammunition to get angry and come back at you.' Mark remembers a particular incident involving Barry Standfield. 'Barry got the ball 30 metres out from goal, bounced it once and waltzed in with his opponent a long way off. In the goal square, he stopped, turned around, showed the ball to the opposition, then kicked the goal. Blighty dragged him straight off. The other mob got the next six goals and beat us. Blight was fuming that Barry had done that, saying it gave them ammunition. I think Barry played one more game, he was dropped and he never pulled on the guernsey again.

'Blighty hated us talking back to the umpires. He said if you're concentrating on arguing with the umpires, you're not switched on or guarding the mark properly. If you made a mistake like pushing your opponent in the back or being caught holding the ball, he would be angry at you until you put your hands in the air on the mark. This meant that every player on the field would see you put your hands up and they'd know you were switched on. Little things like that were pretty clever in playing positive football.'

14

FULFILLING A DREAM

On 31 January 1997, Mark Bickley fulfilled one of his dreams in football when he was appointed as captain of the Adelaide Football Club. The self-doubt about his leadership in the bleak winter of 1996 had been cast aside by the confidence that Malcolm Blight had brought to the club.

The ascension to the captaincy was predictable for a player who had served his apprenticeship with distinction. But the circumstances of Mark's call-up were typical of Blight. His interest in Mark could be sourced back to Bob Boston, the former Port Adelaide player who boarded with the Bickley family in Port Pirie, and who instilled much of the tenacity in the little kid who cried for a game with Solomontown.

Blight tells the story. 'I used to work in a bank with Bob Boston, who lived with the Bickley family for a while and played footy in Port Pirie. When I was in Melbourne playing, Bob would bring a group of friends over from Pirie for the Melbourne Cup carnival, and they'd come out to my house for a barbecue. Max Bickley, Mark's dad, occasionally came on those trips. So when Mark started to play with South Adelaide and then the Crows, I took a bit of interest in him. Even when I was coaching Geelong, I thought he was coming on nicely. When I arrived at the Adelaide Footy Club, I had no hesitation about Mark being captain. It just looked so obvious. But people had seen the qualities in Mark a long time before I came onto the scene.'

Soon after Blight's return to Adelaide, he called Mark to arrange a meeting with him in Adelaide. The two of them went for a long walk along the picturesque banks of the River Torrens. As they strolled along in the heat of midsummer, the conversation was very informal. They talked about football in general, the club, and what had gone wrong in previous years. Mark felt privileged to be asked his opinions and more than a little overwhelmed when Blight asked him to captain the club. 'It was a great honour and I looked forward to the challenge,' Mark said.

Blight says, 'I asked Mark to realise the implications of being captain. I do rate captains and leaders of the club. You can't buy spirit in a football club. You also require good solid citizens, on and off the ground. Mark epitomised those qualities. One of the great things about Mark is that he didn't whinge or complain about his lot in life. Even when training, if I said we were going to do something again, he'd be the first one there. If you moved him during a game, his attitude was, "if that's where the coach wants me, that's where I'll play." He knew that the only way for the club to be successful was to show some character and to be honest. Taking his football ability aside, if you said they were the only two qualities he brought to the club, that would be plenty.'

Blight is wonderfully descriptive in his analysis of how Mark went on to fulfil his duties as leader of the club. 'Duds don't play 200 games and duds don't hold up premiership cups. They just don't.'

From the outset, Mark did not seek to model himself on his predecessors Chris McDermott and Tony McGuinness, two players

Mark (*left*) and David tucked away for the night.

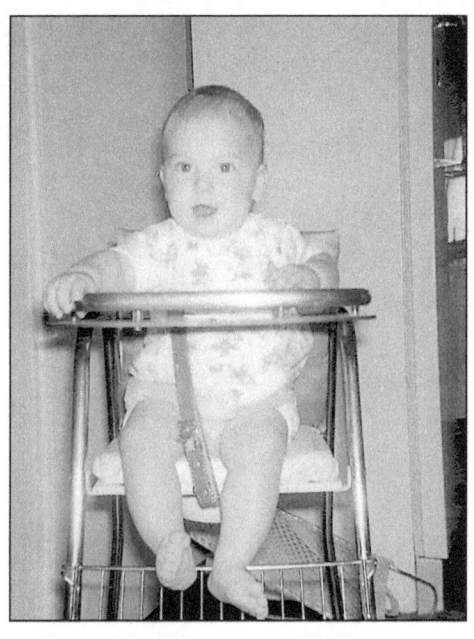

Who would have thought he'd captain an AFL side to two premierships?

Mark, aged four outside the change rooms at Memorial Oval, Port Pirie.

Mark (*right*) and David with their well-worn football in 1975.

Mark (*left*) and David as young players for Solomontown.

Mark on his first day of school in 1975.

Mark's (*front row, third from right*) first year as a player in 1976. His Mum promised him a new pair of boots.

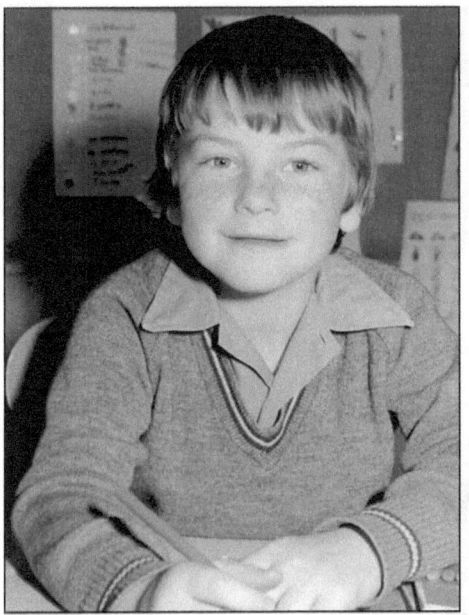

In Grade 3 in 1977.

At age nine, with Bob Boston, wearing Bob's old Port Adelaide lace-up guernsey.

The Solomontown Senior Colts premiership team in 1977. Mark, sitting at the front, is the team mascot. Max Bickley (*centre row, sixth from the left*) in the white T-shirt, coached the side.

Mark and Tanya's wedding day, 1994.

Robert Shaw addresses the players at Victoria Park.

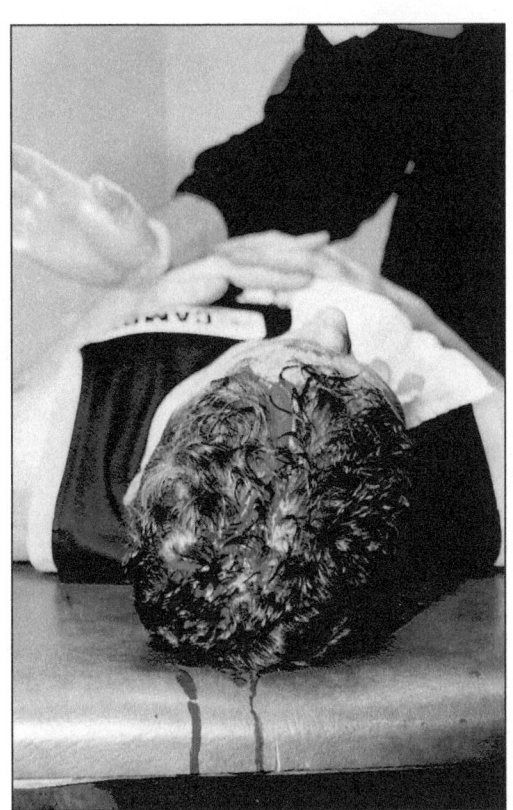

The shocking head injury Mark suffered playing against Collingwood at Victoria Park in 1996. The took doctors over two hours and 37 stitches to close the wound.

The old stagers turn it on for the camera ... 100-game players (*from left*) Nigel Smart, Tony McGuinness, Mark Bickley, Chris McDermott, Ben Hart, Andrew Jarman and Rod Jameson.

The most enjoyable run in football — the victory lap of the MCG after the 1997 Grand Final.

Expressions of absolute joy after winning the 1998 Grand Final.
COURTESY NEWS LIMITED

Crows coach Malcolm Blight grabs the cup with his right hand covering his face.

Mark asks Blight why he grasped the Cup in his right hand. The coach explained that he did not know what he was doing. 'I'd never been there before,' he said.

On the MCG and in darkness after the 1997 Grand Final. Before boarding the bus to leave the ground, the players made a pact to repeat the performance in 1998.

Traffic stoppers ... thousands flocked to the centre of Adelaide to celebrate the Crows' 1997 premiership win.

Broken glass collected from Albert Park Reserve prior to the first Qualifying Final against Melbourne in 1998. The Crows were forced to train at another ground.

Focus on the ultimate prize ... Mark and Malcolm Blight at the Grand Final Parade in Melbourne prior to the 1998 Grand Final.

Mark belting out a handball against North Melbourne.

Congratulations ... Tanya embraces Mark immediately after the Crows' second consecutive premiership.

Mark's parents, Max and Babs, with their son in the rooms after the 1998 Grand Final.

Welcome to the premiership club ... Mark with (*from left*) Mark Ricciuto, Ben Marsh and Peter Vardy.

Malcolm Blight and Mark parade the cup through the main street of Adelaide in 1998.

Grim faces as Malcolm Blight faces the media after announcing he will leave the club at the end of 1999. (*From left*) Bill Sanders, Malcolm Blight, Bob Hammond and Mark Bickley.

Farewells — Mark wishes Malcolm Blight the best after the coach's last appearance with the Crows at the end of 1999. It was also the last game for Matthew Liptak, standing to the left of Blight. Rod Jameson was also farewelled at the end of this game.

The Adelaide Football Club welcomes new coach Gary Ayres (*second from left*).

Chairman Bob Hammond presents Mark with the award for Team Man of the Decade.

Mark bursts through the banner for his 200th game with the Adelaide Football Club.

Mark with his daughters, (*left to right*) Natasha, Shayne and Aleesha.
COURTESY THE ADVERTISER AND BRETT HARTWIG

A famous locker in the Crows dressing room at Football Park. Premiership players, Best and Fairest winners and 100-game players have their lockers preserved for tradition.

Captain Mark Bickley leads the team out of the Crows rooms at Football Park. Note the sign above the door reminding the players of the importance of winning at home.

Coach Gary Ayres fires up his players.

Mark in action in Melbourne with premiership team mate Shane Ellen.

One of the rare pictures of Mark Bickley outside the pack.

for whom he had enormous respect. He was a different person . . . a person who was right to lead the club in that defining period of its evolution.

'I didn't want to clone myself on Chris and Tony, but I did draw on my experiences with them both, especially Chris. In the end, Chris's body was so worn and torn that he was not able to lead the pack as often as he would have liked. But his efforts off the ground were also an inspiration. He used to say that to get the best out of yourself as a player and give the team the best chance to perform well, you had to feel comfortable. For years, I'd seen Chris work so hard to make sure that everyone was happy. If anybody had a problem, he would be an advocate and try to help them out. This was at a time when player welfare officers did not exist. Quite apart from football, Chris would help guys find work and give advice and direction in their lives. Today, a lot of this work is done by full-time staff in football clubs. Those qualities in Chris impressed me enormously. Tony also set great examples with his culture of really working hard on the training track and in games.'

So Mark stepped forward as captain to much fanfare. Nigel Smart was appointed vice-captain and Mark Ricciuto deputy vice-captain. 'My leadership wasn't going to be autocratic. It was a period when we'd lost four or five guys who had played a lot of footy. It meant blokes like Nigel, Mark, David Pittman, Rod Jameson, Matthew Liptak, Ben Hart, Shaun Rehn and myself had to stand up and be responsible for the club's destiny. We'd played a lot of footy for one shot at the finals in 1993. We were pissed off about that and, to a certain extent, apportioned the blame on ourselves. We had to look in the mirror and say we hadn't been doing things well enough. We also knew we had to embrace everything the new coach told us. I wanted to make sure there were six or eight guys who really took on the responsibility of leadership and that's how it worked out. Everyone worked together towards the one goal.'

In Mark's filing cabinet of memorabilia was the sheet of paper on 'The Basics of Leadership', presented to him years before by Wayne Jackson when he was Chief Executive Officer of SA Brewing. The paper featured quotations from famous leaders such as Field Marshal Bernard Law Montgomery, Field Marshal Sir William Slim and General Dwight Eisenhower. However, the quotation that always drew Mark's greatest interest was from Lao Tze, who wrote in 600 BC: 'A leader is best when people barely know that he exists, not so good when people obey and acclaim him, worst when they despise him. Fail to honour people, they fail to honour you. But of a good leader, who talks little, when his work is done, his aim fulfilled, they will all say: "We did this ourselves".'

Mark and his senior players knew the team had to get fitter and train harder. He felt the team couldn't just coast along clocking up games, that there had to be accountability and honesty. 'At the start of 1997, we were at a crossroads.' he says.

As the weeks progressed towards the start of the home-and-away series, Mark wondered whether he should be meeting with the coach more often to discuss team issues. 'When he was captain, Tony McGuinness seemed to meet before every training session with Robert Shaw and John Reid. After six or eight weeks as captain, it occurred to me that I hadn't really gone to meet with Blighty. I went up to him and said: "Should we be having a meeting or something?" Blighty thought for a moment, then said: "No, if we need a meeting, I'll let you know."'

A season of discovery was about to unfold.

15
THE FAMOUS NUMBER 18

Malcolm Blight started plotting for the grand final from his first day at the helm of the Adelaide Football Club. He had met with John Reid at Portsea in the pre-season and, together, they rated the 1997 team as a five out of ten prospect. And, despite the enormous groundswell of public euphoria on his homecoming, his head was well below the clouds. But having acknowledged all of that, his philosophy was that if you didn't have a September dream, why would you turn up?

The team, particularly the new leadership group of players who had notched up around 100 AFL games each, also knew there was major round potential just waiting to be unleashed. Mark says: 'There was a realisation that if we didn't all get together and really give it a final crack and achieve something, the whole thing was going to pass us by. This was particularly felt by players like Nigel, Pitto, Jammo, Darren Jarman and myself. We were getting on in our careers, and if we didn't get some results, we weren't going to be around for long. So, we had to embrace the new coach and his philosophies in order for the club to move forward.'

There is further evidence that Blight's season plan embraced the ultimate game. Having inherited a team with an apparent phobia about its inability to win games consistently interstate, the coach instituted a travelling routine the club would stick by 'win, lose or draw'. Mark recalls how the team had always chopped and changed travel arrangements to determine a routine that would have the players at their best for games. If one routine didn't work, they would change it. 'When Blighty came, he said we'd fly over the day before a match, find an oval, train, come back to the hotel, have a meeting, go to bed and get up the next day for a game of footy. I remember him saying early in the season: "If we play in a grand final, this is what you're going to have to do, anyway. You'll have to come over for the grand final parade on the Friday, so let's have a routine right from the start. This is the way it's going to happen, no matter what.'

Consistency in training and travelling arrangements were all part of Blight's grand plan and it had a settling effect on the team. Blight told the players the training program would be the same throughout the year. He liked having every Thursday off to play golf, and he thought the players needed a break, too. So they knew that they could plan ahead for the whole season with confidence, knowing that Thursday was a day of enjoyment. Mark says this was a great move. 'Realistically, Blighty probably didn't expect us to make the grand final in 1997. But that's what you play for. It's no good having a routine, and then stepping away from it for the most important game of your life.'

It took the team a while to get used to their game plan, because it was a step away from what they had been doing previously. Blight told them: 'Look, if you keep trying to do what I want you to do, we'll have success, but it's going to take time to be ingrained in your psyche.' This was a steadying influence, particularly in the first few games when the Crows weren't playing well. Blight continued to reassure them that they were improving and that they were about to turn the corner. Different tactics were employed, but the fundamentals never changed. It was driven into the team not to overuse the handball. He wanted them to play direct football, trying to kick goals quickly and pressuring opponents by putting scores on the board. He wanted the ball long to centre half forward, then have players run into that area to crumb the pack. The players worked hard to embrace the game plan as quickly as they could.

In the opening game, Adelaide easily accounted for Brisbane, one of the powerhouse clubs of the previous season. But the team's confidence took a severe nosedive over the next fortnight, with losses to Richmond at the MCG – the game that generated the 'pathetic Pittman' furore – and to Carlton at Optus Oval.

Round four was the first of the so-called showdowns against Port Adelaide, who were playing their first season in the AFL. There was intense hometown rivalry between the supporters of each club. Football Park was a sellout, with 47 256 fans filling the stadium and hundreds of thousands more watching a live telecast around the State. Adelaide was expected to win this first encounter, despite the fact that its injured list included three club champions – Shaun Rehn, who was anxiously awaiting his comeback from his second knee reconstruction, Matt Connell and Matthew Liptak. Other absentees were David Pittman, Simon Goodwin, Darren Jarman, Clay Sampson, Matthew Robran, Shane Ellen and Aaron Keating, each of whom were to play in Adelaide's first premiership team. Port Adelaide won the game 11.17 to 11.6 and Crows fans retreated in embarrassed silence. *The Advertiser* was damning in its report the next day.

> *Not surprisingly, a sombre pall fell over the West Lakes home of the Adelaide Crows last night. There was no joviality from the Crows' meeting room deep within the multi-million dollar training facility, unlike three weeks ago when the occasional echo of laughter had emanated from the Monday night meeting with coach Malcolm Blight. That was*

after an impressive first-up performance and 36-point victory against Brisbane. But three weeks of frustration and losses have followed, culminating in the 11-point humiliation from Port Adelaide, and the club is again being given a 'please explain' by the public.

Captain Mark Bickley, who has been with the club since its formation in late 1990, last night defended Adelaide against charges it cannot succeed because it lacks any sort of history as a club. 'If you really want to draw something from it you can. Port has the opportunity to use its history, and they make a strong point of it,' he said. 'It has its advantages, but when you're a new club obviously you can't draw on it, so you don't try.'

Bickley maintained tradition, by its nature, is not created overnight. But he conceded there was a strong feeling among the players that they had let their supporters down. 'They have stuck with us and they are obviously going to be copping a bit of flak, and we feel for them as well,' he said. 'The only way we can really repay them [the supporters] is to get our heads down on the track, come back and have two wins in the next two weeks.'

The spirits of the humbled Crows players were certainly at a low ebb when they arrived at Football Park for training on Monday night after the loss to Port Adelaide. This was not supposed to happen under Malcolm Blight. Many players felt they had let him, themselves and their supporters down. Every member of the team expected an arctic blast from the coach. But what they had not predicted was the thinking of the man who had been through many winters of victory and vanquish, and all the associated emotions at the highest level of the game.

Mark was amazed at the coach's mood when the players filed in for training. 'We were expecting to cop a blast, but when we walked into the meeting room Blighty had written the number '18' on the whiteboard. He asked: "Does anyone know what 18 stands for?" Finally, we worked out that there were 18 games left in the season before the finals. Blighty said, "We've won one and lost three. There are 18 games left. Why panic when we're still embracing a new philosophy. We're getting better at it." It was a pivotal piece of coaching that reassured everyone. He told us not to listen to the doomsday people, and instead reassured us and gave us confidence.'

Blight remembers how forlorn the players looked when they arrived for Monday night training. 'The club was pretty distraught, and I don't think the players knew what they were going to get. The meeting didn't last long, then we went out and played footy. Oh, I did play a tape of an incident in the game that lasted about 20 seconds. Two of our blokes tackled a Port player and then another three Crows players jumped on top. There were five against one. It was a football club gone silly, and I said to the players: "Come on, we don't need to play like that."'

Blight felt that Port Adelaide was just another team. 'I'd been in the system a long time. The team had *not* been in the system a long time, nor had the people in charge of the club. So when everybody else was forlorn about being beaten by Port Adelaide, it didn't bother me in the least. It was just another four-point game. You learn from it, and get on with the season.'

Blight had played in two premiership sides with North Melbourne, each time after poor starts to the season. His experience was invaluable at a time when the Adelaide Football Club could have succumbed to its self-doubt. In that context, the humbling loss to Port Adelaide was the turning point of the season, along with the steadying influence of a master coach who knew how to repair broken spirits.

The following week in Melbourne, the Adelaide Football Club conquered the Western Bulldogs in its first win on Victorian soil for more than a year. This was the match in which Shaun Rehn made his comeback, and the resurgent David Pittman made his first appearance since the 'pathetic' incident. The following week, the Crows lost to Collingwood at Victoria Park by one point, despite having 28 scoring shots to 19. After that loss, they had five consecutive victories.

The players had embraced the Blight game plan, but from time to time he was ferocious in his criticism of those who erred. He was tough on himself, too. If he attacked a player verbally during the intensity of a game, he was just as capable of winning back that player's confidence. Mark remembers one occasion when Blight said he had not helped anybody by yelling and screaming. 'He said he'd been out of the game for a while and had forgotten how hard it was to get a kick! He was pretty selfless and quite often prepared to take a lot of the blame when we were not playing well.'

In Round 15, the Crows beat St Kilda – the club it would face in the grand final – and four weeks later staked its revenge against Port Adelaide. Critics noted how the team's stamina allowed them to run over opponents, and much of this fitness was credited to the influence of Neil Craig. Blight's lieutenants – assistant coaches Darel Hart and Mark Mickan, the first club champion – were great stalwarts, along with match committee members John Reid and Terry Moore.

Despite a loss to Essendon in the last minor round match, Adelaide entered the finals in fourth position. Every confrontation in the major round was a potential knockout. After such a grinding effort to make the finals, the prospects of ultimate success were daunting. But in his own controlled manner, this was the party that Blight had booked. In Victoria, they sniggered about the Crows. Meanwhile, the players who faced Essendon in the 1993 preliminary final quietly vowed to cast off that baggage. This was going to be one hell of a ride!

16

A FOOTBALL LIFE

Tanya Kuchel hated football. A legal secretary who enjoyed hockey, the only football matches that attracted her attention were grand finals, because they generated so much publicity. Even then, she'd usually swap her support from one team to the other halfway through the game. However, the march of the Adelaide Football Club into the final series of 1997 completed something of a journey of discovery for the girl who swore she'd never get tangled up with a footballer.

In 1991, Tanya was enjoying a night out with her girlfriend, Jo Firth, at Lennie's Tavern, near the foreshore at Glenelg. Jo was there with her boyfriend, Matthew Liptak, one of Glenelg Football Club's best young players and a recruit of the Adelaide Football Club. As the band played and the drinks flowed, Jo introduced Tanya to Matthew's mate, Mark Bickley, a Port Pirie boy feeling his way in the big smoke.

'When I was introduced to him, Jo said Mark was a footballer. I said "yeah, yeah!", because I thought they were having me on.

Surely, I thought, there was no way that Jo would introduce me to a footballer. This is really sad, I thought, but later in the night we were looking at a team photograph of the Crows on the wall. Mark pointed to one of the players and said: "That's me." I looked at it but I still didn't believe him. It was a good night but, to be truthful, I wasn't too keen at that stage.

'A few days later, Jo rang and asked me along to a Crows match. I told her I had been at home sick, and shouldn't be going to a footy game. She said, "Tanya, I've got nobody to go with . . . get rugged up, we'll watch the game, and as soon as Matt comes out, we'll go home." So I went, but I was petrified that my boss would see me at the football and that I'd get into trouble. After the game, Matt came up to the concourse area in the grandstand, where we were waiting, and right behind him was Mark. It was such a set-up. Then we went into the clubrooms and I was dressed in a woolly jumper, an old jacket and sneakers. Everyone else was dressed beautifully and I thought to myself, "This is just great!" But Mark and I got on really well. He was so funny, and I found him attractive.'

Suddenly, Tanya found herself in a club within a club, comprising the wives and partners of Crows players. It was alien territory and, in the early days, if people asked her a question about football, she admits they did not get a very intelligent answer. However, she was committed to scaling the learning curve. 'I didn't have much of a choice about becoming involved in the game. The girls were all thrown into it together, and I was so lucky that I knew Jo. In the first year or two, there were a lot of functions because the club was trying to get everyone together. It was great fun.'

But the culture that initially had set Tanya against footballers was very evident as the players basked in the spotlight of an adoring public. She tells how they felt like there were two groups of people . . . the players and the girls. 'It was forbidden for a player to hold his girlfriend's hand, or to show any affection. The guys got revved up by their mates, and they had this stupid system of fines if they were caught kissing or holding hands with their girlfriends. It was really hard, because you were treated one way in private and another in public. It was hard and a couple of times I felt like I'd had enough of this football thing. We depended on our girlfriends, since we were all going through the same thing. But, essentially, Mark was always good towards me, and after a year or two the guys came to their senses.'

Tanya's disdain of the football culture did, however, erupt at the Brownlow Medal count of 1992. 'We had a great night and retired downstairs to the bar to have a few drinks with Chris McDermott, Tony McGuinness and Stephen Kernahan. Mark then disappeared for a while and I went looking for him. It was really late and I wanted to go to bed. I found him in a corner talking with Bob Hammond, Malcolm Blight and Leigh Matthews. I went up to the group with Mark's jacket in my hands and said: "Come on Mark, let's go." He turned around and replied: "Tan, go away ... I'm talking to important people here." I looked at him, then put the jacket right over his head. The next morning I told the other players and they gave Mark heaps.'

Mark and Tanya became engaged in 1993. One of her early accomplishments was breaking Mark out of his habit of watching television in bed before going to sleep. 'Apparently, he'd done this since he was 13 years old. The first night I moved in with Mark, I got into bed and he switched on the television. I asked him what he was doing, and he simply said, "Watching TV." I told him, "That's what the lounge room is for." We haven't had a television on in the bedroom since.'

Among Tanya's attendants at their wedding in 1994 was Jo Firth, and Mark was joined by a showcase of AFL footballers – Chris McDermott, Scott Lee, Ben Hart, Tony Hall, Tony McGuinness, Matthew Robran, Mathew Liptak, Nigel Smart and Rodney Jameson. Also among the wedding party were two of Mark's closest mates from Port Pirie – Jason Turner and Scott Aldridge. The media rejoiced in the celebrity AFL wedding, reporting how Tanya looked spectacular in an off-the-shoulder, ribbon lace, full-length, slim-fitting gown with rosettes around the shoulders, long sleeves with scattered sequins and a detachable cathedral length tulle train. If Tanya knew little about the finer points of football, Mark knew less about the description of her wedding dress, enhanced as it was with a 'gold and pearl crown held by a fingertip veil'.

'All I know was that she looked spectacular,' he said. 'It was the happiest day of my life.'

In the months before the marriage, Tanya had nursed Mark after he broke a bone in his foot. It was difficult handling his frustration. 'He was irritable, especially in the lead-up to a game when he couldn't play. He was really short with people. But we coped, and he was really spoiled at home. We were due to pave our backyard when he was injured, so instead of Mark, it was my mum and me on all fours laying the pavers, while he sat in a deckchair and gave directions.'

It was Mark's head injury in 1996 that really scared Tanya. 'I went to the airport to meet him, and when the guys came off the plane they just looked at me and shook their heads. I knew that he'd been injured and that he'd had stitches. Nigel told me he had about 30 stitches. I imagined they'd be nice, neat little stitches and that it would not be so bad. Then when he showed me the injury, I felt the blood drain from my body. It was awful. He amazed me – he should have been in hospital. Yet he played the next week.

'I realised then that nothing I could ever say or do would stop him from playing, despite his injuries. There have been so many times that I have asked him questions like: "Why are you playing? Why are you going out there?" He injured the ligaments in his little fingers in the pre-season period one year. He played the full year like that because the club wanted him to play. His fingers got worse every week. If they had been operated on at the time they were injured, he would have missed a few games, including Ansett Cup matches. Now he can't straighten his little fingers. But that's the way it is and I have learnt to live with it.

'It's not for me to say, "Here I am, and this is what is going to happen." Mark has been playing football all his life. It is his job. I can't come along and tell him yes or no, or lay down the law. It is an occupation and it has its risks. He accepts those risks and I guess I have to as well. I cringe, but often when he goes down on the ground, I just urge him to get up. If he's back on his feet in a few seconds I know he's all right.'

In July 1996, Tanya gave birth to their first daughter, Shayne. Two sisters – Natasha and Aleesha – followed in March 1998 and June 2000.

'When I think back, Mark was pretty relaxed about me going into labour with Shayne. It was five o'clock in the morning and he wasn't convinced I was having contractions. He sent me out to watch TV. Within half an hour, I was doubling over in pain. Mark decided there was plenty of time for him to have a shower, and in the end I staggered into the bathroom and screamed at him to get out. I got in the car and told him to hurry up with my bag and to take me to the hospital. After what seemed an eternity, he came to the front door and yelled out, "Where are my jeans?" I nearly had the baby then and there. Luckily, we got to the hospital at about half-past six and the baby arrived at 9 o'clock. Mark is always quite relaxed if it doesn't involve football!

'I remember how we created a furore when I went on 'The Footy Show' with Mark just before his 200th game. I was expecting Aleesha at any moment. Somebody asked me what I'd do if I went into labour on the day of Mark's big game. I replied that I'd expect him to play and that I'd have the baby on my own, if necessary. We heard next day that people were ringing radio stations in Melbourne and Adelaide saying that I had the wrong attitude and that Mark shouldn't miss the birth of his child. Others were ringing saying he shouldn't miss his 200th game. It was quite bizarre.

Nobody knew that we had already arranged to have the baby induced so Mark would be at the birth. I suppose if we'd told people that they'd complain that I didn't let her birth come naturally. People think you are public property. I would never have expected Mark to miss his 200th game. As long as he is there for the girls for the rest of his life, that's all that matters.'

Over the years, Tanya has come to grips with being a footballer's 'widow', looking after the children while Mark spends hour upon hour at training or away playing. She accepts that sometimes football has to come first. She has learnt to cope with the fear of football injury and the fluctuating temperaments of recovery. And she has had to endure invasions of privacy and rudeness from so-called supporters. Often they would be introduced as a couple, then Tanya would be ignored by people who sought only to converse with Mark, or to have him sign autographs. 'When we go out, a lot of people come and say "G'day Bicks", which is fine. Others yell out things like "Go the Power!" and you think to yourself, "Gee, I haven't heard that one before."

'People say "Oh well, he gets paid for that", or "It's the price you have to pay." I guess that's true in that football is Mark's career and he has worked extremely hard. But it would be nice if people adopted the attitude that he's with his family, so let's just leave him alone. Many people are polite and they are also embarrassed if they ask him for an autograph. However, I get really annoyed when opposition supporters heckle Mark when the girls are with us. He doesn't hear it half the time, but I do. We have to choose where we go as a family. For instance, we won't go together to the Adelaide Show, because Mark is approached too much. It is disappointing for the girls that sometimes their dad can't go with them and have the fun I had with my family at the Show.

'I know the coach's wives had to put up with a lot. I didn't really get to know Robert Shaw, but his wife, Gail, was lovely. It was terrible that she and their kids had to put up with so much from so-called supporters. I was disgusted to be a South Australian watching the pain they were going through in Robert's second year with the club. Their house was pelted with eggs and their girls were being teased at school. Wherever they went they'd run into a barrage of abuse. Neither he nor his family deserved that sort of treatment.'

This was the reality, the downside. Mark's career meant the imprisonment of a strict regimen that dictated when he could be with his family, have a night off, go out for dinner and even what he could eat. But, for Tanya, the positive will always outweigh the negative. She is a beautiful but tough woman who does not cry easily. However, in 1997, she surprised herself more than a little with the tears of joy that flowed for her husband and the realisation of his dream.

As the Crows geared up for their second finals campaign, Tanya cast her mind back to the preliminary final loss against Essendon four years earlier. 'All the players' wives and girlfriends flew over and we were sitting directly opposite the Essendon players' wives and partners. At half-time, we were on top of the world, saying to each other that we had it won. The others looked pretty sad and downcast. Of course, in the last half the game switched around and it was their turn to cheer and yell. It is a strong memory.'

Tanya, a football convert, knew Mark was out to avenge that loss. As the pillar of support behind the captain of the Adelaide Football Club, so was she.

17

AGAINST THE ODDS

As if there wasn't enough incentive already ... before the first qualifying final against West Coast Eagles at Football Park, word had spread that the opposition considered Mark Bickley a 'one-dimensional counter-puncher'. If football is played as much between the ears as it is on the ground, it pays to be careful with what comes out of your mouth. The Eagles were to eat their words, just as a few St Kilda players were to discover the full sting of unwise utterances a few weeks later.

In the first qualifying final, the Adelaide skipper was the heart and soul of the Adelaide Football Club. He played a fearless, tenacious and inspiring game of football that clearly made him best on ground. His fanatical attack on the ball and body, and his willingness to hunt and chase resulted in 20 first-half possessions against his highly rated opponent, Dean Kemp. Blight was the first to applaud him, saying that if you get your skipper doing that at the start of the game, it usually flows on to the rest of the players. Analysing the game for the media, Graham Cornes noted that Mark's collision with Brett Heady showed exactly how a strong commitment to the ball could do as much damage to an opponent as any malicious or illegal intent.

The 33-point demolition of the Eagles, considered the biggest intimidators in the game, signalled the intent of the Crows not to yield any ground in the 1997 finals series. While the players were unswerving in their determination to win the qualifying final, Mark believes the victory was also inspired by the experience and genius of their coach, qualities that were illuminated time and time again in the momentum of that joyous month of September 1997. For a start, Blight kept the expectations of the masses out of the dressing room, reminding his players to work from one week to the next, to overcome one hurdle before thinking about scaling the next.

The qualifying final against the Eagles took place on a windy, blustery day. 'Well before the game, we went out onto the oval to see which way the wind was blowing. Malcolm had always said if we win the toss and there's a strong breeze, kick with it. But this time, Malcolm pulled me into the coach's room and said, "I'm thinking if we win the toss, we might kick against the breeze." His methodology was that in finals, there tend to be nerves and the first quarter can be pretty scratchy. He thought that perhaps we might be able to hold the Eagles a bit, then once the steam had gone out of it in the second quarter, we could use the breeze to our advantage. He asked me my thoughts, and I said it made reasonable sense. At our team meeting before the game, he asked how everyone felt about it. We were all with him. Fortunately, I lost the toss. Imagine the crowd if I'd won the toss and pointed into the breeze! Anyway, we got our wish and, as it turned out, we attacked consistently and outscored them in the first quarter. It really did set up the game.'

Adelaide broke a seven-year hoodoo of being unable to beat the West Coast in daylight. Deflated Eagles coach Mick Malthouse conceded in staccato fashion, 'Adelaide was too good for us. We had opportunities, didn't take them. Adelaide did.' Blight cautiously responded: 'It was fantastic, wasn't it!'

It was a hard-running and aggressive group of young men who worked throughout the second week of the finals series to confront Geelong, the team that Blight had coached and taken into two losing grand finals. His rival coach in the second semi-final was Gary Ayres. The win against the Eagles set up another homeground advantage for the Crows, and Geelong's record at Football Park was not impressive.

The frenzied crowd witnessed an epic contest with Geelong leading by eight points at three-quarter time. While Blight had instilled self-belief in the players, the stamina run into muscles, lungs and hearts by fitness coach Neil Craig began to make itself apparent, as the home side clawed back the advantage. It was a quarter of desperate defence and frantic probes into the forward lines, in the middle of which was the resolute and inspiring presence of Shaun Rehn. The crowd at Football Park was gripped by drama and apprehension as Peter Vardy, in an inspiring cameo, gathered the ball from an impossible position and kicked under severe pressure for goal. This came at great cost – a broken collarbone that ended Vardy's season.

Perhaps most of all, the game will be remembered for a last-gasp effort from Geelong's Leigh Colbert. Late in the game, Colbert soared high over a pack of Crows defenders and crashed to the ground with the ball in his hands. He was within easy kicking distance of the Geelong goals. Shoulders slumped, and a heavy pall of silence descended on the Adelaide players, surrounded by gob-smacked disbelief in the terraces and grandstands. Incredibly, the umpire did not pay the mark and he took the ball from a heartbroken Colbert. In a game where goals were like diamonds, he and the Cats were denied what seemed rightfully theirs. It broke their spirit and Adelaide won by eight points. Mark and the more senior players had fulfilled their destiny of playing in another preliminary final.

* * *

Sometimes you get your hand to a ball, or you deflect it, or you tackle someone and hold on by your fingernails. These types of little things can sometimes change the face of a game, and when the games are big enough, they can change people's lives.
These are the words of Mark Bickley, who, in his own summation, plays the game on the strength of his commitment, rather than the sum total of his natural skills.

I believe you can make your own luck. Really good players can actually focus on the ball spinning through the air and determine which way it is going to bounce.
Malcolm Blight, the former champion footballer and a coach who never speaks highly of himself.

Adelaide has done nothing to dispel the theory relating to home finals, with victories over the Eagles and Geelong which, in my view, was extremely unlucky.
Kevin Sheedy, an interested observer.

I'll resign from every form of football media if the Bulldogs can't beat Adelaide.
Sam Newman, former footballer and entertainer.

In the soul-searching lead-up to the 1997 preliminary final against the Western Bulldogs at the MCG, Malcolm Blight's belief in the team was contagious. But if he had begun to sniff the aroma of freshly mown couch grass on the last Saturday of September, all he did was sneeze. His edict was to stick to the basics and enjoy the ride. It wasn't so much what had changed about the Adelaide Football Club on its finals crusade. It was more about what hadn't changed. The supporters' expectations rose on a thermal of hope and anticipation, but across the border, there was little expectation that the Crows, despite begrudging acknowledgement of a coach who had served his time, would be capable of spoiling an all-Victorian football party. Enter into the equation the inertia of a rearguard, including Shaun Rehn, Ben Hart, Mark Bickley, Nigel Smart and Rod Jameson, who were among the 'returned servicemen' of 1993. This absorbing cocktail of emotion and influence filled the MCG on preliminary final day – Saturday, 20 September. St Kilda, the team who had finished on top of Geelong, West Coast, the Western Bulldogs and Adelaide at the end of the minor round, waited imperiously to take on the winner in the grand final.

Former champion Richmond rover and television commentator Kevin Bartlett described it as 'one of the great wins' in finals football. After two quarters, the Western Bulldogs led 10.6 to 4.11 and it appeared that the Adelaide Football Club's major round odyssey was coming to a crashing end. The tragic run of injuries had continued, from Peter Vardy the week before, to Tony Modra, who had to be stretchered off the MCG with a serious knee injury. In the change room at half-time, Blight worked on the whiteboard – Nigel Smart to full forward, Rod Jameson to full back, Troy Bond and Andrew McLeod into the centre square, Aaron Keating into ruck, Shaun Rehn to centre half forward and an out-of-form Matthew Robran to the bench. Having determined the positional changes, Blight urged his players to win the third quarter. To do so, he said, would put them in a position to win the game. As the Crows duly followed their instructions to move within 23 points at three-quarter time, Modra limped back onto the sidelines on crutches. His worst fears had been confirmed.

At three-quarter time, the coach was more confident. He told the team to build on the momentum of the third quarter, and he switched Darren Jarman to full forward. The defining moment of the game came at the nine-minute mark of the final quarter. Tony Liberatore had a snap shot at goal and, believing it had gone through, hurled himself onto the shoulders of his teammates. But their celebrations were premature, as the goal umpire signalled a point. Liberatore, lying in a cradle of limp arms, looked up in disbelief. Mark, who was among the better players that day for the Crows, realised it was going to be a game of inches.

'I was right behind Liberatore when he had the shot at goal. The ball didn't spin and it was almost horizontal as it went over the post. It was so close. Then we saw Liberatore jump into players' arms. The goal umpire was in the perfect position. If it had been called a goal, I think that would have been enough to stop our momentum, enough for them to go on and win the game.'

There was another incident late in the last quarter, when Tyson Edwards desperately chased and smothered a kick by Chris Grant. This stopped what would have been a certain goal. Mark says of that moment, 'Sometimes, in situations like that, a player can find that extra bit of energy, that extra inch, that can change the course of a game. It is an awesome feeling.'

Suddenly, there was a groundswell of red, blue and gold. The Bulldogs fought desperately to regain their composure, but the Crows surged forward time and time again. Leading the charge were the players of '93 – Bickley, Smart, Rehn and Hart. Young guns Andrew McLeod and Kane Johnson were in overdrive. The crisis had unleashed pace and skills that they may not have even known they possessed. With Chad Rintoul and Matt Connell, they weaved through packs and defied the frenetic, flying tackles of their opponents. With less than two heart-stopping minutes to play, Johnson booted the ball lace out to Darren Jarman on the run – a perfect pass. With customary poise, Jarman's goal put the Crows in front and their army of supporters leapt to their feet, screaming, urging, pleading, crying. The MCG echoed and rumbled with the drama. It was the same story in front of thousands of television sets back in South Australia.

* * *

Tanya, pregnant with Natasha, could not bear to watch. The preliminary final loss in 1993 was still chiselled in her memory. 'I was at Mum and Dad's house and they were watching the game on television. I couldn't stand it. I felt sick with nerves and went outside to weed the garden. I actually broke out in a nervous rash, but it disappeared after two or three days.'

The Crows won by two points. Graham Cornes, the man who steered the club into its first finals campaign, rejoiced in his role as a radio commentator and newspaper columnist. Carefully tickling the alphabet for *The Advertiser* after the victory over the Bulldogs, a smile beamed in with every turn of phrase as Cornes lifted a heavy veil from the past with his poignant and visionary words.

Suddenly, the run came through the midfield from Bickley, Hart, Goodwin and Johnson, the use of the ball improved dramatically, and Jarman and Smart exploded into action in the forward lines. In less than ten minutes, Adelaide throttled the life and the spirit out of the Bulldogs and – to the disgust of the Victorian football secessionists – stormed into its first AFL grand final. It is worth recounting that the atmosphere in the predominantly Victorian press box at that moment at the MCG was one of absolute shock. They could not comprehend that the team of which they had made an art form of ridiculing had dared to triumph. Praise for Adelaide's performance was not graciously forthcoming. It was more that the Bulldogs had lost it, rather than Adelaide had won. The psychological demons of 1993 have been exorcised in the most emphatic fashion. The club has suffered much since that match, but maybe it was meant to be part of the larger picture. Certainly, as Bickley indicated with his post-match comments, those players who remembered that experience were never going to let another preliminary final opportunity slip from their grasp.

Adelaide's best three were McLeod, Rehn and Ben Hart, with honourable mentions to Peter Caven, Matt Connell, Jarman and the energetic, big-hearted, but decidedly underdone Aaron Keating. Now, to bring us all back to reality, it's on to the grand final where Blight has a few psychological demons of his own to exorcise. One senses, however, that he knows his next grand final will not be a losing one.

In Port Pirie, Babs Bickley was packing the bags for Melbourne.

18

THE PINNACLE

The Crows players did not realise the enormity of their achievement until their homecoming from the preliminary final. Their training runs took place in front of thousands of fans, cheering every twist and turn, clapping every mark and kick. The parochialism of football had once prospered in the suburbs when each team played for the pride and reputation of its own district. There were distinctions between the teams: between the 'haves' and the 'have-nots', blue-collar workers against white-collar workers. Catholics versus the rest. Enemy lines were main roads rather than State borders. The Adelaide Football Club had marketed itself as the 'team for all South Australians'. In the excitement of grand final week in 1997, it seemed that all of South Australia was urging the club to succeed. The clarion call to victory was as loud in fishing towns, on farms and at the very doorstep of the Outback as it was around schoolrooms and kitchen tables in Adelaide. Politicians in election mode went along for the ride. It was a marketer's dream and just a few kilometres from the Football Park home of the Crows, the Port Power hierarchy and their supporters watched with a curious mixture of envy and admiration. In some Port Power quarters, there was begrudging support because, at the end of the day, it was a South Australian side playing a Victorian side for football's greatest prize. The last time a South Australian side had faced such a monumental challenge was in 1963 when the State team triumphed at the MCG against the might of Victoria.

In the midst of the hullaballoo, Malcolm Blight was a picture of calm. This was his September dream, and in many ways he was reliving it. Mark recalls how the coach seemed to know everything that would happen in the week ahead.

'The day after we beat the Bulldogs, we had a bit of a chat. Blight said, "Well done. It was a great comeback. Now, when you get home, be prepared to have 20 messages on your answering machine. I bet one of them will be from someone you haven't heard from in ten years, and they'll be wanting tickets to the grand final." When I got home, Tanya told me the phone had been running crazy and that I had a pad full of messages. Mostly, they were from well-wishers, but there was one from an old schoolteacher, asking about the chances of getting some grand final tickets. Blighty had predicted it. But, more importantly, he really stressed that we should enjoy the week, soak up the atmosphere, but at the same time keep in the back of our minds that there was a job to be done. He told us we were good enough to do it. From the start of grand final week, he said that nobody was to mention the word premiership. The word was outlawed.'

The coach then told the players something they would never forget. It was an intriguing, mystery message that he would repeat at the same time the following year, but against a different team. Mark can't remember the exact words, but it was something like: 'We'll have a plan in place to win it. Leave it in my hands.'

Blight had been through it so many times before as a player and as a coach. He seemed relaxed, but the players were walking around with eyes like dinner plates. It was all so new. Darren Jarman was the only player in the side who had played in a grand final – when he was with Hawthorn.

Hundreds of letters and messages of support poured into the Adelaide Football Club. Many were addressed to Mark Bickley from people in Port Pirie. One came from David Hookes, the former South Australian cricket captain and vice-captain of the Australian cricket team. It said:

> *'Just a quick note to wish you and the side all the best. It's going to be the greatest sporting day of your life, so savour and enjoy everything about it. Just stay calm, positive and aggressive and the scoreboard will look after itself. Again, Baz, congratulations thus far – just one step remaining and, in the words of American President Theodore Roosevelt during the Second World War, "Accept the challenge without reservation or doubt, risk the depression of losing so that you may experience the exhilaration of victory." Good luck. You have the entire State supporting and willing you to victory.'*

Melbourne, in fact, became a sanctuary for the Adelaide players, far from the pressure of expectation and adulation, and close to the derision that was as apparent in street talk as it was in the media. Mark recounts how it was a relief for them to get to Melbourne. 'We flew in Friday morning, booked into our hotel and then went to the grand final parade. This is how Blighty predicted things when we were flogging our guts out pre-season. I'm not saying he had a premonition, but his confidence and surety seemed to steer us on an inevitable course. He certainly made us believe in our ability and our destiny.

'After the parade, we could return to the hotel without being pestered, hounded or harassed. In fact, after lunch, we had a bit of time on our hands. The only obligation was a team photo at about four o'clock and then we were going down to the Junction Oval to train. I was a bit buggered after the parade – pent-up nervous energy I guess – so I just lay down on my bed and fell asleep. I was woken up by the telephone ringing. It was Barrie Downs, our team manager. He said: "Mark, we're all down in the ballroom for the team photo. What the hell are you doing? You're the only one not here." I was shitting myself. I had to get all my clobber on quickly and race down, thinking I'd cop it from the coach for holding everyone up, but Blighty just laughed.'

Following the team photograph, the Crows had a final training run at the Junction Oval. Later, as they returned to the hotel, Mark ran into West Coast Eagles coach Mick Malthouse. 'I'd met Mick a couple of times previously, and he came up to wish me all the best. He said the team that settled down first had a huge advantage, and he told me to make sure the boys were calm at the start. Then he said: "I actually think you'll win." I asked why and he responded: "Because you've got a coach who has been there before and experienced the whole thing. I think that's worth five goals."'

The club flew all the wives and girlfriends to Melbourne for the grand final, and Mark saw Tanya briefly on the Saturday morning of the game. He then went for a walk in Albert Park. 'I started out on my own and sat on a park bench having a quiet read of the *Footy Record*. Peter Caven then turned up, and we sat together for about an hour, just talking about the day and what had happened during the year. It was an opportunity to have some peace and to be reflective, something we would not have been able to do in Adelaide without being holed up inside. We then strolled back to the hotel and turned on the television. A TV crew was with two or three of the St Kilda players while they were eating breakfast. Then I saw David Sierakowski and his father being interviewed at a breakfast somewhere. His dad, who was a member of the last St Kilda premiership team in 1966, was asked if St Kilda could win, and he said he wouldn't mind if it was by a point. David chipped in and said something like, "You don't have to worry about that, we'll win by seven or eight goals!" I was quite happy to hear that because they were doing heaps of media stuff, and we were all pretty controlled and relaxed.'

Max and Babs Bickley had driven to Melbourne for the grand final, but had not caught up with Mark before the game. They settled early at the MCG, but Babs was rattling with nerves. 'I couldn't eat or drink anything, so I just sat there and waited. I remember at one point turning to Max and saying, "Imagine the Crows winning the grand final. To think where Mark has come from – where we've come from – and watching him hold the Cup." Max said, "It would be bloody magnificent." I was so emotional. I just started howling, and later on I think Max did, too.'

The consensus of opinion was that St Kilda would be too good for the Crows. Yet in reaching the grand final, Adelaide had beaten the second, third and fifth sides and the Saints had accounted for seventh and eighth. However, the Crows injury list was extensive. Modra was in a wheelchair, Trent Ormond-Allen had glandular fever, Peter Vardy was nursing a broken collarbone and Mark Ricciuto had not recovered from a groin injury that kept him out of the entire major round. The walking wounded also included Simon Tregenza, who had struggled to overcome a knee reconstruction, and Matthew Liptak, the 1996 club champion, who was on crutches.

Blight's experience, incisive analysis, calming influence and tactical genius were telling factors as the side prepared to burst onto the MCG. In the captain, he entrusted the final words to the players.

'Before the game, Blighty told us not to get carried away with all the pre-match entertainment on the ground. He said there were about 18 minutes from the time we ran on to the ground to the start of the game. He said, "Just go out there and see if you can spot your mum and dad, or your wife or girlfriend in the crowd. Look around. Soak up the atmosphere. Enjoy all the pre-match stuff."' Blight instructed the team to go to Mark after the national anthem, so he could run through the key points of the game plan. Mark spoke to the team about making sure they settled down first, being hard at the ball and not giving away free kicks, taking chances and running off to create the loose man.

To be sure everything went to plan, Blight had one final instruction. 'I'd arranged with Mark to get the boys together just before the start of the game. I told him to get them all to look towards me in the coach's box and I'd know they were all switched on. This he dutifully did, and then they were off.'

What St Kilda had not expected was Blight's master plan. In Shane Ellen, he had conjured up a full forward who had played his football career in defence, previously kicking only three goals in the AFL. And he put the youngest member of the team, Kane Johnson, a raw 19-year-old, on the Brownlow Medallist, Robert Harvey.

In the desperate pressure of the first quarter, the Crows lost two players – Rod Jameson with a torn hamstring injury and Clay Sampson with a thigh injury. The grand final was over for them. Shane Ellen kicked two goals for the quarter and the Crows were two points ahead at the first break. Early in the second quarter, Barry Hall managed to get away from Peter Caven three times in a matter of minutes, and the Saints went 16 points clear. Some of the Crows' big-name players – Bickley, Hart, Smart, Robran and Rehn – were not firing. Blight benched Rehn and set Aaron Keating loose. As Caven ran off the ground with blood gushing from a gash above his right eye, the news was all bad for the Crows. At half-time, St Kilda held sway by 13 points.

Once again, Blight dug into his bag of tricks, making changes that turned the game. In the third quarter, Andrew McLeod switched from defence to centre, and Jarman moved into the forward lines. Ellen returned to his customary defensive role and Rehn regained touch in ruck. The Crows began to reel in the Saints and suddenly the momentum swung, with Ellen kicking a goal off the half back flank. The forward line rose to the courageous efforts of the defence and Rehn exerted enormous influence. Jarman marked on the run and his goal put Adelaide in front. At the last break, the scores were Adelaide 11.11 to St Kilda 9.13.

Blight had planned his three-quarter time address in the grand final from the day after the stunning victory against the Western Bulldogs. As he walked onto the ground at the last break in the biggest game of the year, he knew the Crows had regained psychological ascendancy, and he knew they had the stamina to run over the opposition. As 99 645 people milled in nervous expectation around the ground and millions watched live on television, Blight seemed to be on a plateau above the drama. Mark believes he was simply enjoying himself, in the knowledge that he was realising his dream. 'He had always told us to set targets for ourselves in each quarter and never to think too far ahead, or preoccupy ourselves with the final result. Yet, in that three-quarter time address, the rules changed. The previous week, he said he'd kick anybody up the arse if he heard them mention the word premiership. Yet, with the most important quarter of football in our lives about to be played, he said we were half an hour from that premiership, and that we could talk about it as much as we liked after the game. He said, "Just go out there and do it. After the siren, you will experience the most exhilarating three minutes of your life." He'd saved this message for the last thirty minutes of the season.'

The final quarter of the 1997 grand final was dominated by the Adelaide Football Club. Rehn controlled the ruck and consistently held up St Kilda attacks. Jarman, taken from the field when playing for Hawthorn in the 1991 grand final, was out to prove that he would not 'choke' in the biggest game of the year. Indeed, the last quarter was the Darren Jarman show. Three sensational goals came in quick succession and the Crows were heading for a five-goal lead. Shane Ellen ran from the back line again, swooped on the ball and kicked his fifth goal of the match. Jarman scored another goal, then another, with Troy Bond booting one more, and Smart the eighth for the quarter. St Kilda sank in despair and Blight leaned back in his chair in the coach's box. This, he had said, is why you bother to turn up at the start of every season. When the final siren blew, the score was 19.11 (125) to 13.16 (94).

Crows supporters danced in the streets in Adelaide and around the terraces at the MCG. On the ground, the players fell onto their knees with fatigue. Mark was physically exhausted. 'I was battling to stand up. In the last half, we kicked fourteen goals and eight straight in the final quarter. But I didn't really believe that we had it won until the 27 minute mark. Nigel kicked the last goal with about five seconds to go, and I remember putting my arms above my head and saying, "We've really won it now." I looked around and the crowd was going crazy. There were a million things going through my mind – knowing that I was a premiership player, an enormous sense of relief, excitement and uncertainty about what would happen next. I thought about being up on the dais and holding up the premiership cup. It is the ultimate dream of every kid who ever pulls on a pair of boots.

'I was consumed. Years of hard word had come together. I couldn't believe what was happening. We were in each other's arms and rolling on the ground with tears and laughter. The first person I hugged was Andrew McLeod. I was just so happy for him. He had the ball in his hands when the siren blew and the umpire tried to get it from him. Then I ran up to Blighty and Reidy, who had brought me down from Port Pirie.

'The emotions were melting all around us. The win meant different things to different people. Shaun Rehn had done so much to be able to play and he had an enormous influence on the final. Simon Goodwin had played only about ten games and he was sensational, and so was Kane Johnson. These young guys were our future. Then it was different again when I looked over to Mark Ricciuto, Peter Vardy and Tony Modra. Words just failed me because I could see the personal disappointment behind their joy for the team. There were guys like Bill Sanders and Bob Hammond who really shaped the club and I felt enormous pride for them too.'

Blight speaks from experience about the winning feeling immediately after the final siren in a grand final. 'That brief period after the final siren is something special. It's as if somebody comes along, taps you on the shoulder and says: "You're it!" There is an incredible adrenalin rush that comes from somewhere, and you feel like you're eight feet off the ground. As a player I got it, and I must admit it was almost as good as a coach.'

Blight and Bickley hoisted the premiership cup and the crowd roared. For the coach, it was a moment of enormous satisfaction. 'The club had set itself up as the pride of South Australia, which was quite right. But I'm not a political person. I just like the game of footy. It was really about watching the young blokes enjoy themselves, watching people around you like the property steward and the team manager who had been there for years. I felt a lot of enjoyment for them.'

In the grandstand, Tanya Bickley was overwhelmed with emotion. 'When Mark ran on to the ground, I was bawling my eyes out. I said to myself, "This is ridiculous, it's only a football match." But he had achieved his dream. He had reached his goal and I was so proud of him being out there and being captain. I was on edge the whole game and so superstitious. I was clutching a Coke cup and every time I put the cup down, St Kilda would get a goal. So I had this tight grip on the cup, and didn't shift position. When Mark held up the cup, the tears were rolling down my face. I could not believe that I cried so much. It is unthinkable for me to do that. But I'm sure Mark's mum, who was in the crowd, would have been crying a lot more than me. After the game, I saw Mark in the rooms and I cried again. He made a beeline for me. Later I rang my mum in Adelaide and she told me people were celebrating in the streets. It was strange, because Melbourne was so quiet after the game.'

Newspaper reporters seized on comments from Crows players and officials, delirious with their achievement.

The greatest feeling was the first fifteen seconds after
the final siren sounded.
Shaun Rehn

*Malcolm Blight being appointed the coach was the
first turning point for the year.*
Nigel Smart

It was just beautiful.
Kane Johnson

*The turning point of the season was losing the Port game.
After that, we had some great performances and some
great wins in Melbourne.*
Matthew Robran

*Ben Hart was just sensational and Andrew McLeod –
how about his final series? We heard a lot of people
say we were going to get flogged and weren't a worthy
opponent, so we took that on board.*
Darren Jarman

I don't know what to say. It's just unbelievable.
Andrew McLeod

*Malcolm said it's the last quarter of the year. Go out
and enjoy ourselves.*
David Pittman

*We won today, and I know the players have got to take
the credit, but I'm telling you we won because we
had Malcolm Blight coaching.*
John Reid

Malcolm Blight did not have a chance to talk to the players as a group amidst the euphoric scenes in the dressing room at the MCG. About half an hour after the game he faced about 50 journalists and cameras. Next to him was Andrew McLeod. Swinging on his chest was the Norm Smith Medal for the best player on the ground in a grand final. The Adelaide Football Club's publication, *A Crows' Decade*, reports on the questions put to Blight and his responses.

How does it feel to finally win a grand final?

Fantastic. To win four finals in all the circumstances . . . I would like to think it would go down as one of the great wins in the history of the game, particularly as we lost two players in the first quarter. Jameson and Sampson couldn't come back on, so we were struggling early and I can honestly say I thought 'Oh no, here we go again.'

After three grand final losses at Geelong, does that finally get the monkey off the back?

'It's just a whole new beginning for me. I suppose most of the well-wishers, apart from family and people at our club, were people from Geelong, including Ron Hovey and Gary Ayres . . . most people at Geelong took time out, including the property steward, and that was very touching.'

Can you remember a side with so many low-profile players?

No, but I love them dearly.

Misty rain fell on the MCG in the twilight after the grand final. The wives, girlfriends and well-wishers had departed and the grandstands were empty and silent. Malcolm Blight gathered the players together and walked them down the race onto the oval. Mark remembers the eerie feeling he had walking onto the arena that only hours before was overflowing with people and emotion. 'It was quite dark, apart from the odd light here and there in the grandstand. So there we were – the coach, the runner, all the players and one or two trainers. We were dressed in blazers and ties to go to the grand final reception at the Melbourne Tennis Centre, but Blighty wanted to get a photograph on the ground before we left – a photograph when nobody else was around. After the picture was taken, he looked at us and said, "Let's make a pact. Tonight we make an appointment to do the same thing next season." '

19

TRIUMPH AND REFLECTION

At the Melbourne Tennis Centre that night, Mark was in a reflective mood as he analysed his own season. He'd gained more possessions than any other player in the club. But he was not satisfied with his performance as a player in the grand final. He had gathered six kicks, two marks and two handballs and he had been overshadowed by his opponent, Nathan Burke. However, his courage over the ball and six ferocious tackles hurt St Kilda, and helped close down a half back flank. At the Melbourne Tennis Centre, he at last had the opportunity for a quiet chat with Blight. 'David Hookes was hosting the grand final reception and each player was being introduced to the crowd. It started in numerical order – Darren Jarman, number three – and continued from there with the captain and coach to be introduced last. Hookesy interviewed the players, so there was some time to sit back with a can of beer and relax. Blighty and I were sitting down on the floor, leaning against the wall. I said to him, "This is fantastic, and I don't want to detract from the whole thing, but I'm a bit disappointed that I probably had fewer possessions today than in any other game all year."'

Blighty was genuinly concerned about what I said to him. He said, "Don't do that to yourself. I couldn't have been happier with your performance as captain during the year, and not everyone can play well on grand final day. It's about the team, and your performances during the year helped us get here." It was reassuring, but I was still uneasy about it. Then he said, "Look, stop worrying. After the grand final, the Melbourne papers have a rating for every player. If you're in the winning team, and you played the whole game, the worst you'll get is five out of ten. By tomorrow night, someone will come up to you and say you should have been in the best players. Stop worrying."

'So we went out to be presented to the crowd and did our stuff. The night passed, and at about two or three in the morning, we finished up at the Crown Casino. A newspaper vendor was out the front, so I quickly grabbed the *Herald Sun* and told a few of the boys what Malcolm had said. Sure enough, the paper had rated each of the players and under the name Mark Bickley, it said something like, "Nathan Burke had the better of him in the first half, but he had a strong physical presence and tackled well. Rating five out of ten." It was that funny. Then, of course, a couple of the papers the next day had me in the best players. By Sunday night people were slapping me on the back telling me how well I'd played. Blighty was right, again.'

For Tanya, the premiership party at the Melbourne Tennis Centre was a mixture of fun and frustration. 'It was a huge party, but some of us were pregnant, including Lee Jameson, Sophie Pittman, Nicole Caven, Rachel Koster, Sue Jarman and myself. We told the boys, "You've got to do this again next year so that we can stay out all night, too!" They were having such a ball, and all we wanted to do was get back to our rooms and go to bed.

At Adelaide Airport, the premiership players were to discover the impact of their achievement. As the aircraft taxied onto the tarmac, a fire engine showered it with water. The proverbial champagne cork had been popped. Rod Jameson reached out of the cockpit window waving the premiership cup, and an enormous crowd roared its approval. It was reminiscent of the pubescent worship bestowed on The Beatles in sleepy Adelaide in the 1960s. There were screams of delight and tears of joy, but instead of starstruck teenagers, the swarming crowd comprised men, women and children who really, really wanted to be there. It was an all-embracing football phenomenon, a demographic that defied convention, a delighted crowd decibelling that South Australia was now the epicentre of the football world.

Mark and Tanya walked off the plane into pandemonium. For a man who had just played in an AFL grand final, the surging crowds raised a mild sense of trepidation, not so much for himself, but for his pregnant wife. 'There were people everywhere, so we had to be ushered through a side door to get out of the place. The road leading out of the airport was lined with people and when we stopped at the traffic lights, our car was completely surrounded. We couldn't drive off because people were trying to get autographs. It was a crazy scene.'

What awaited the Adelaide players at Wayville Showgrounds was even more extraordinary. About 25 000 delirious fans had gathered for an official welcome-home reception where the coach and players, already bleary-eyed from hard celebration, were to be introduced to the crowd.

Mark and Tanya drove home from the airport and, after a quick shower, Mark headed for Wayville. He was among the first of the players to arrive. 'I was standing around with a can of beer in my hand and our team manager, Barrie Downes, came up and reminded me that our timekeeper, Wally Smith, was gravely ill with cancer at Ashford Hospital. Wally had been with the club from day one, but he was too sick to make the grand final. Barrie had promised that if we won the premiership, he'd bring the cup in to the hospital. With a few hours to spare before the official reception, Barrie asked me to go to the hospital with him. So off we went. We stuck out like dog's balls walking into Ashford on a Sunday with the premiership cup, and we found Wally. He was very sick, but delighted that we'd come in to see him. He wanted to touch the cup. When we went to leave, a lot of people were waiting outside the door to ask if we'd show the cup to their loved ones, so we made a bit of a tour of the hospital. I think it brought some cheer into the lives of some pretty sick people.'

In fact, Mark did not realise how much of an impression he made that day at the hospital. Quite some time later, he received a letter from a lady named Joan Wilkinson of the Adelaide suburb of Manningham. It read in part:

Dear Mark

I apologise for not writing before this and thanking you for the great service you did for me. It was at the Ashford Hospital when you took the premiership cup to show a sick friend of yours. I saw you and asked would you mind saying hello to my husband, who was very ill. I'm sure it was the turning point. With your help, you allowed him to hold the cup. I can't thank you enough for your kindness.

The next few days were exhausting, with a Town Hall reception, street parades, parties and official functions.

Tanya, with baby Shayne running around at her feet and a baby on the way, had also been run ragged in the celebrations. 'People didn't quite understand. It was great to have everyone so happy, but at the same time, we'd had no sleep and everyone was exhausted. I remember at one stage we'd just got back from a function desperate for a sleep, and phone call after phone call came from radio stations. I answered one call and the person asked for Mark. He asked who was on the line and I said, "Some f*!#%$* radio station." I didn't realise, and they didn't tell me, but I was live on air. I don't know what they did to cover it, but I can look back on it now and have a laugh.'

It was not until the Wednesday after the grand final that Mark caught up with his parents. There were many tears; Mark had inherited his mother's genes in that department. The premiership captain was speechless. 'Sometimes the unspoken word is more powerful than the spoken word. When I saw Mum and Dad, it was more about big hugs than anything else. I knew they'd be happy. It was something they'd cherish for the rest of their lives, so it was great to think that I could do something that would make them proud of me.'

Another letter arrived soon after. It read in part:

Dear Mark

Congratulations on leading the Adelaide Crows to their first historic AFL premiership. You now rank among the small band of elite players and captains who have had the honour of holding aloft that very elusive trophy. Your place in Australian Rules history, and that of Port Pirie, is now assured. I know success did not come easily. Your commitment, the long arduous hours of training, sacrifice and just plain courage, together with your football skills, took you to the pinnacle of the AFL. Well done. Once again, you have brought great fame and credit to your family, the city of your birth, and yourself. The community is very proud of your achievements and would like the opportunity to express to you their admiration when the demands on your time permit. Looking forward to you accepting our invitation to a civic reception and returning to Port Pirie: the home of the Adelaide Crows captain.

Ken Madigan
Mayor
Port Pirie City and Districts Council

The Adelaide Football Club, pursuing its promotion of the Team For All South Australians, sent the premiership cup and players on a Holy Grail Tour of the State. About 2000 people braved heatwave conditions to greet the players in Port Pirie's Memorial Park. Mark was absorbed into the crowd, laughing with people he'd known all his life. It reminded him a little of the annual smelters picnic, when the Pasminco workers and their families relaxed in the shade of gum and peppercorn trees between egg and spoon and three-legged races, hot dogs, warm cordial, and dusty cricket matches. So much had changed in his life since leaving Port Pirie nine years earlier. He liked to come back now and then to be with his family and friends. But Adelaide had become his home. It was where he wanted his own children to grow up.

Babs Bickley accepts that her youngest son will never return to Port Pirie to live. But she constantly reminds him of his roots. 'When he does come home, he absolutely loves it. When his friends come around he's the same old Mark. I think sometimes when he's down there in Adelaide he gets up himself a bit, but I just say to him: "Remember where you came from. You're a Port Pirie boy, so don't go getting too jumped up." He just laughs because he hasn't changed.' Max Bickley agrees. 'He's often gone down to the Sollys club on a Friday night to see his mates – including Pinkie, Porkie, Bushpig and Monkey – and ended up washing dishes out in the kitchen for Babs and the ladies.'

In the weeks after the 1997 premiership, Mark was on the verge of a major business decision that he hoped would consolidate his future and provide financial security for his wife and children beyond the football years.

20

ONWARDS AND UPWARDS

The media continued to show interest in Mark. Channel 9 in Adelaide signed him up to comment on football for its nightly news service. But he was on the lookout for a business investment. Mark sought advice about his financial planning from his manager, Ian Gray.

'I spotted an advertisement in the newspaper about an AFL store franchise in Adelaide. I rang Ian to say that I had seen something that was of interest to me. He said, "Oh, don't worry, I've already booked you on a flight to Melbourne tomorrow to meet with the franchise people." He was thinking for me. In the end, I was able to secure the franchise for two stores in Adelaide. It was a great opportunity that would not impose too much on my time for my family or training, while giving me the flexibility to plan for my future.

'Ian had the acumen and experience to steer me in the right direction. It took a huge load off my mind, allowing me to concentrate on my family and footy. He advised me about buying a home and even did the bidding on my behalf at the auction.'

It was an incredibly exciting time for the Adelaide captain. The club had won a premiership, he'd purchased a business with confidence in its future, and Tanya was expecting their second baby. 'I was in a position where my family relied wholly and solely on me. I had to plan everything carefully.' While he received expert advice in his investment decisions, the responsibilities of the captaincy rested quite easily with Mark, notwithstanding the extra burden of public expectation that often fell on his shoulders.

'I was only the third guy to be named captain of the Adelaide Football Club and it was a great privilege. I have enormous respect for my two predecessors, so to be in their company was an honour. At the same time, we have a team that is admired by people all over the country and emotions rise and fall on the performance of the team. I realised the importance of being chosen as one of the people to guide the team in terms of performance and the image that it projects. When I was appointed captain, Blighty had a word with me about the responsibilities, and he mentioned things like loyalty, discipline and setting the right example. On some occasions, the captaincy is a political and diplomatic role. You have to be very careful what you say because you're asked for an opinion on everything – from what you have bought for Mother's Day to how you'll vote in an election. As captain, you are the spokesperson for the team and you have to remember that the club has an image to uphold. It has sponsors who pay a lot of money to be a part of that image, and you have to protect it.' Mark had enjoyed the captaincy from the beginning. He relished the opportunities he had to meet and talk to many new and interesting people, from politicians to captains of business. He also had the opportunity to meet sick and underprivileged children and this was very special to him.

Despite its impositions on family and privacy, football has also been beneficial for Tanya and the girls. 'It was hard at the start with Shayne because Mark was still working at the brewery. He'd leave home at 6.30 am, train at 7.00 am, go straight to work, then to training after work and get home around 8.00 pm when Shayne was asleep. It got to the stage that she wouldn't go to Mark. She knew he was Dad, but she wouldn't let him nurse her. I made him take two weeks off work so that he could spend time with Shayne and get to know her. But that all changed when he became a full-time footballer because there was more flexibility, allowing training later in the morning and having him home earlier in the evening. There have been some difficult times, but football has given us great opportunities in life. I think we're so lucky, and it's all due to Mark's hard work.'

Ian Gray has had no small part in Mark's personal development. He recalls a turning point. 'Mark had been appointed captain, and I think it might have been one of his earlier speeches before the 1997 season. The occasion was the player–sponsors' dinner, an important event at the start of the year when it is customary for the captain to address those attending. For some sponsors, it's the first personal association with the players.

'Bicks got up and gave a nice little speech to everyone, then he sat down to polite applause. The next day, he came into my office and I told him that I remembered a quotation from Winston Churchill, who said, "The best impromptu speeches I ever give are those I spend most time preparing." I told Bicks the speech he had given at the player–sponsors' dinner was terrible, and that he hadn't thought about or formally recognised the people attending – from the chairman of the club to board members, management, players and sponsors, who were paying a lot of money. I asked him to think about the importance of preparing speeches. He reacted very well, and we talked about the things that he needed to develop. He was more than ready to accept the challenge of improving himself.'

Since then, Mark has undertaken courses in public speaking, media, leadership, small business and computing. Ian describes how willing he has been to take the next step and apply his knowledge. 'Mark is now a highly respected and very competent public speaker, and he enjoys a similar reputation when working in the media, particularly television and radio. He has become a very astute businessperson who applies himself to the tasks at hand, and he's very active in managing his own share portfolio.

'Bicks matured as a person from a good country lad to a professional footballer, businessperson and media expert. Yet, he still remains very much Mark Bickley. His success and achievements have not gone to his head in any way and he remains very approachable and well liked. He's also well equipped for life after footy. He is in a position to choose whatever direction he would like to head, whether it is in the media or business. He also has an open mind towards coaching. Mark's investment in South Australia's first AFL stores was a great success, with the Crows' premiership providing an enormous sales boost of AFL-licensed merchandise.' Ian Gray recalls how diligently Mark applied himself to the job, having invested a considerable amount of money. 'His learning curve was very steep. Until that time, he knew little about business. He asked a lot of questions and really got involved in the management. He committed a lot of time to being in the stores.'

Ian has always been impressed with the time Mark spends serving customers and talking to them about football, describing him as gracious towards and tolerant of people who simply come into the store hoping he's there.

'There is a quote from a famous golfer, I think it was Gary Player, that I really think reflects a lot about Mark's character and his willingness to apply himself. Player had just won a major tournament, and a lady evidently went up to him saying, "Congratulations, Gary. That was a very good round, but you certainly had a good deal of luck." Player turned to her and said, "Thank you madam. But it's amazing that the more I practise, and the more I try, the luckier I get!" That's Bicks.'

While high in praise for his protégé, Ian also reveals a little about what he describes as Mark's wicked sense of humour. 'I remember a trip on my boat when I had a few of the Crows boys aboard, including Mark, Nigel Smart and Kym Koster. We were anchored one night off Kangaroo Island, and Bicks decided he'd teach us all to play an evil game that he called 'bullshit poker'. The rules were that if you were caught bullshitting, you had to skol your drink. Many hours later, I remember hanging over the side of the boat – which is pretty rare for me – and I looked inside to see Bicks, Smarty and Kym nearly killing themselves with laughter, and just sipping their beers. I blamed the wine yet, on reflection, I realised that, in fact, Bicks had told the most porkies, but was caught the least. I claimed to be the opposite, but also realised all those guys were too experienced to be caught bullshitting, and they also knew how to pace themselves with their drinking. However, I must say, after that event their fishing stories weren't to be trusted.'

21

AND AGAIN?

As the Adelaide Football Club prepared for the pre-season of 1998, every player had his own share of responsibility. Each was determined that people would not say that he was content with one premiership, and not hungry for a second. Interviewed by the media at the time, Mark spoke about motivation after missing out on a place in the winning team. 'Tony Modra, Mark Ricciuto, Peter Vardy, Matthew Liptak and Simon Tregenza – all great club men – missed out in 1997, and that gives us significant motivation to do it again with them in the team. Malcolm's philosophy is that a team has to keep improving. If we weren't to make the finals in 1998, we could hardly say we've developed as a club.'

So, the campaign was on again. If the Adelaide Football Club earned respect in 1997, it was going to demand it in 1998. It was all a matter of momentum and Blight was prepared to let fitness coach Neil Craig raise the bar. With all the fanfare after the premiership, the team did not start training until late October, about three weeks later than the previous year. Mark welcomed the hard work. 'I was looking forward to it for two reasons – getting back together with the guys, and getting into physical shape. It had been a fairly extensive lay-off and we'd enjoyed ourselves, so it was good to get back into the routine of training.'

There were very detailed records of the squad's fitness and their times from the previous year. In the first training session for the '98 season, Blight told the players to make sure they gave themselves the best chance; they needed to have a solid fitness base. He wanted to ensure that by Christmas, they would surpass their fitness levels of the same time in the previous year. His aim was for the team to believe they were fitter and better prepared. The difficulty was that they had three weeks less in which to do it, so they had to work hard after their high-spirited celebrations.

In the pre-Christmas period, Blight focussed on one-on-ones with players, particularly those who had been recruited or drafted into the club. His priority was that they learnt and understood the Adelaide Football Club game plan. At the same time, he moved around, spotting deficiencies in players' techniques and advising them on how to improve. As Neil Craig got them fit, the coach was very much in teaching mode. Mark is not a subscriber to the theory of premiership hangovers: when for inexplicable reasons teams with unchanged or improved playing ranks struggle the year after they achieve the ultimate glory. Besides, Blight did not leave the door ajar for such negative thoughts. 'He would not accept guys who were prepared to rest on their laurels and think that what we had done in 1997 was good enough. He said there were about 15 guys in the squad who had not experienced a premiership, and they'd be going flat out to make their mark. There was also a handful of guys who, for one reason or another, had missed out on playing in the premiership side. Mark Ricciuto, especially, was really driven. He'd won our Best and Fairest in 1997 and was an All Australian, so he was very disappointed to miss out. Instead of wondering what could have been, he just got out there on the front foot and did everything he could to make sure he was in the firing line again. That's the mark of the man.'

The Crows also had to endure the claims of detractors that they had been lucky in 1997. There was an undercurrent of opinion, primarily among those with axes to grind, that Adelaide had not come up against seasoned finals campaigners. No credence was given to the fact that the club went into the 1997 grand final without two All Australians – Mark Ricciuto and Tony Modra – along with Peter Vardy and Matthew Liptak. Mark recalls how the players were keen to silence the critics. 'We were all determined to show that people had not given us the credit we deserved. We'd developed a genuine belief in ourselves and in the coach's philosophies. In terms of fitness, we knew we could come over the top of teams, and that had been very clearly demonstrated in the finals series.'

Three days before the opening game of the 1998 season, Tanya gave birth to Natasha. As with Shayne's birth 20 months earlier, Mark was present for the delivery. 'It was a treasured moment,' he enthused, 'an unforgettable experience.'

From the tenderness of the maternity suite, the Crows captain was then cast into a ferocious contest against Carlton in the opening game at Optus Oval. This was the type of attack the premiership side had to expect. Adelaide lost by 10 points, but the following week dominated Fremantle at Football Park. A grand final replay against St Kilda loomed in round three, and Adelaide knew the Saints would come out bursting with vengeance. Blight was keen to soak up the pressure and have a good win. Chasing St Kilda's 32-point lead at three-quarter time, the Crows started the last term with Rehn and Ricciuto on the bench. As the team sank towards defeat, they were joined by Smart and Jarman. In the wake of the 22-point loss, Blight defended his action in creating what was labelled the 'million-dollar bench' suggesting the form of the players did not match their star reputations. Mark, who was among the best players in the first three games, said it was a clear message from the coach. 'He felt a few of the senior players were running their own race. This was a new year and he said that we all had to perform week in, week out, or face the consequences. Everybody was on notice.'

Blight looked ahead to the showdown against Port Adelaide. 'To be 1–3 would be as low as you'd want to get at this stage of the season,' he mused. 'With Port at 1–2, it's set up for a big derby.' One point separated the sides at three-quarter time in front of a sellout crowd at Football Park, but Port's straighter kicking and more polished performers around goals proved decisive in winning 11.7 to 8.16. It was a bad loss, but Mark remembers little panic. 'We'd been there before. It was a repeat of the previous year. We were so keen to win that we gave away some silly free kicks. The previous year, Blighty wrote number 18 on the board after losing to Port to signify that there were 18 games to go. The message got through, and he didn't need to do it again. He was just trying to get us refocused. It was almost as if we needed to be behind the eight ball to rise to the challenge. When people started suggesting the first flag was just a freak, it was enough to stir us into action and we clawed our way back into the eight. It was a scratch and a scrape, but we'd always set our sights on making the eight. We knew if we got there, we could be really dangerous.'

In the last three minor round games, the Crows were teetering on the edge of the eight. But there were some exciting performances to come, and very clear signs that the club was rising once again at the crucial time of the year. In Round 20, Adelaide beat Geelong at Shell Stadium, its first win on that ground. It then lost by 13 points to North Melbourne at Football Park before beating West Coast at Subiaco, for the first time on that oval. The minor round ended with the Crows in fifth position.

The round 21 game against North Melbourne was pivotal, because Blight had watched like a hawk from the coach's box, and evidently he spotted prey. Mark remembers him coming into the players' room after the game looking buoyant and almost excited. 'He said to the players, "Look, I'm disappointed we lost. But, I saw something tonight. If we play them again this season, we'll beat them." At the time, we all thought it was a big statement. North had won seven or eight in a row and they were a couple of games clear on top of the ladder. But Blighty sounded so sure of himself. He had seen something about the way they played and he was very confident we could beat them if we met them again. He didn't say what it was, only that he would let us know when the time was right.'

The team's major round defence of its title got off to a disastrous start in the first qualifying final against Melbourne. There was a bad omen on the eve of the game when the club tried to train at Albert Park Reserve. Instead of a freshly mown expanse, the ground had been top-dressed and laced with shards of broken glass and metal. There were mumblings of sabotage, but they weren't very loud. While Albert Park was off limits, the MCG was no more welcoming the following day. In fact, it became a killing field, with Melbourne slaughtering the ruling premiers by 48 points. Mark went into that game quietly confident. 'We hadn't lost a final the year before, and we entered the major round in pretty good form. But, at the same time, Melbourne had come into the finals at a rush and we treated them as a danger side. On the day, we were terrible and they were great. Tony Modra played poorly in attack and he was switched into defence late in the game. After the game, the coach had a crack at a few players. He could cop losing, but could not accept it when he thought players were not making a contest. He was upset that he'd put a side that wasn't competitive on the ground in a final. Blighty was really fired up and indicated that two or three players were going to be under pressure to hold their places in the side. Matty Liptak, who had a lot of injury problems, had come back in and he really wanted to make an impression in the finals. But he pulled a hamstring that signalled the end of his season.'

Adelaide was in the finals race by a thread. To advance, it had to beat an in-form Sydney at the SCG in a do-or-die second semi-final. Blight's anger was fearsome, Mark recalls. 'He could be angry during a game, but it would usually be different by Monday. This time you could see the anger was still burning fiercely when we rolled up for training on the Monday. During the day, he'd called Mods into his office and told him that he was being sent back to West Adelaide. When we arrived at training, Mods stormed into the change room with a big cardboard box, emptied out his locker and ripped his 100-game plaque off the door. We thought, "Jeepers, what's going on here?" Then Blighty came in and explained what was happening. He said that rather than unsettle the side just before the game against Sydney, he had decided to tell Tony early in the week.

'That week, we trained really hard and the coach was intimidating. He was still angry. He told us, "This team will not go out of the finals in straight sets. If you guys let two chances slip, there's something wrong in the make-up of the players." He intimated there could be wholesale changes, and everyone was on edge.'

When the players faced the Swans in Sydney, they were jumping out of their skin to make sure they won. It had been raining all week and the ground was a bog. They ran out into what felt like a tropical downpour, and there was no wind. The rain was coming down in buckets and there were explosions of fireworks in the sky. The smoke wasn't clearing. The crowd was yelling and screaming. The atmosphere was eerie. Ricciuto ran up to Mark and said, 'Mate, this must have been what it was like in Vietnam!' Mark laughed, but soon gathered his thoughts. This was no time to be laughing.

'It was a hard slog, but we won it 14.10 to 10.7. McLeod, Jarman and Vardy – especially Vardy – were spectacular and it was a magnificent effort. What a difference a week makes. Blighty was so happy. It seemed that all the anger had washed away.'

After the game, Mark was interviewed by Channel 7. Asked about the week ahead, he replied something along the lines of: 'This week, it will be about recovery. We've had two away games, a hard week on the track after the dismal performance against Melbourne, and playing in a bog in Sydney. This week will be all about freshening up.'

They drove out to the airport on a bus and when they arrived, Blight asked officials and others to get off, leaving only him and the players. He said to them, 'I am so happy with the way you responded today. You showed some real character as a footy club. You had a really hard week on the track leading up to this game, and I honestly believe the way we trained was the key to winning the game. So, this week, we're going to do exactly the same thing – the same intensity and the same competitive work – to prepare for the preliminary final against the Western Bulldogs.'

Mark says that you could have heard a pin drop in the bus. 'We were all completely shagged. Later, a few of us were talking in the airport and the consensus was something like ". . . everything he has told us in the past has been right . . . we've got to go with him." This was the respect we felt for Malcolm Blight. We had faith in him. Then again, there was no choice. It was his way, or the highway.'

Vardy had kicked six goals against Sydney; he was hungry for the premiership medal that had so sadly eluded him in 1997. Mark says that no one appreciated that Vardy had a bruised heel and it was getting worse each week. One of Blight's rules was that unless the players trained flat out on Wednesday night, they couldn't play on the weekend. As they advanced in the finals, Vardy was having painkilling injections, just to get out on the training track. You can only do that for so long, according to Mark, 'because the injections dull the pain, but they don't fix the injury. But then there were only two short weeks to the grand final.'

The penultimate game of the season was an opportunity for the Western Bulldogs to avenge their defeat in the preliminary final the previous year. It was that game, the dismal memory of a two-point disaster, that formed the foundation of their psychological assault on the 1998 premiership. That foundation quickly crumbled against the punishing Adelaide attack. By half-time, the Crows were nearly six goals clear; by three-quarter time, they had almost doubled the Bulldogs' score; and by the end of play, the difference was 68 points. Mark walked off the ground delighted and inspired by the desperation of his teammates, especially Ricciuto and Vardy, and the awesome seven goal display by McLeod. 'It could not be denied,' he says. 'Adelaide was a hardened finals campaigner with its sights set on the biggest premiership favourite for years – North Melbourne. The performance against the Bulldogs was unbelievable, and it gave us a lot of confidence going into the grand final. This time, the critics had no ammunition. It was going to be a showdown between two teams that knew what it was all about.'

At Tullamarine, after the preliminary final, Blight once again asked the players to stay on the bus. They all thought, 'Here we go again!' He told them that they'd won because they were super-competitive, and that was because of the way they were training. He then added, 'This week it won't be as long or arduous on the track, but we'll stick to our training regime and it will be competitive.' His message was that this would be a hard, but enjoyable week. Essentially, his final message before the players flew home was, 'It's what we play for . . . now bring on the game.'

On either side of the battlelines – which for the huge majority of supporters was the State border – the expectations were high. The Victorian football public rallied behind North Melbourne, as it had done the previous year with St Kilda. Another success by the imposters from Adelaide could not be contemplated – in fact, it would not be tolerated. North Melbourne was too good, they said. This was a team that knew how to win grand finals. It was inconceivable that the side that finished at the top of the minor round could lose.

In Adelaide, hope was the strongest ingredient in the many recipes for victory conjured up by the Crows supporters. From mid-week, carloads of fans headed east and once again the red, blue and gold army descended on Melbourne. At Football Park, Malcolm Blight walked around with a spring in his step. Perhaps it was nervous energy, but it was unlikely. This was the week that he enjoyed most in the game, particularly when he could test the elasticity of his own football brain. The smile he often wore should have provided ample warning to North Melbourne that the plan he had brewed would, at the very least, make the 1998 grand final a classic contest.

The Crows players knew he had a strategy. He'd talked about it when North Melbourne beat the Crows in round 21. But, Mark believes, nobody 'twigged' until the team meeting on the eve of the grand final. 'It had to do with Pagan's Paddock and the North Melbourne players getting behind our defenders, then sprinting towards goal. Blighty actually saved his secret plan until we were in Melbourne on the Friday night. He said, "I've always said that defenders must stand in front or alongside their opponents. I've always wanted the team to play from the front. But tomorrow, I want our defenders to play from behind." He wanted to stop North Melbourne from rushing forward towards goal and kicking long to Wayne Carey in one-on-one contests. This strategy was also designed to stop their running players from picking up the crumbs of the contest between Carey and his man, and running unhindered into goal.

'I'm not sure if Blighty was the first coach to come up with this idea against North Melbourne,' says Mark, 'but it was so interesting, because he had always encouraged defenders to play in front, never behind. He had the courage to change everything around on the eve of the grand final.'

With his experience from the 1997 grand final, Mark was more organised. He'd arranged for his mum and dad to come into the rooms after the game, along with Tanya. The previous year, the families of other players enjoyed the champagne-soaked atmosphere in the dressing room after the game, but Mark had been too preoccupied to arrange things for Babs and Max. They had stood behind a fence, desperate for a glimpse and a word with their son. In 1998, Mark also booked a table for guests at the post-match dinner and invited his parents, his brother, David, and his wife, Judy, Tanya and her sister, Jackie, and their dad, Rod. Also on the invitation list were two of Mark's closest mates from boyhood days in Port Pirie – Scott Aldridge and Jason Turner.

Sometimes, it's the little things. Mark was thinking about tossing the coin to gain a psychological advantage against North Melbourne. At the start of the 1997 grand final against St Kilda, he shook hands with his opposing co-captains Stewart Loewe and Nathan Burke and, as the umpire threw the coin, Mark called heads. He always called heads! As the coin came to rest on the grass, the umpire picked it up carefully and declared there was no head. It was a commemorative coin which on one side featured the Olympic rings, and on the other an engraving of the Great Southern Stand. Loewe seized the opportunity and instantly claimed the winning toss. Some time after the premiership, Mark and his manager, Ian Gray, were reminiscing about how he had no hope of winning the toss. Ian recalls, 'We decided to have a bit of fun with Wayne Jackson, who has a property in the south-east of South Australia, not far from my vineyard and winery at Padthaway Estate. I hunted around coin collectors in Adelaide and told them of my mission, eventually finding an 1897 Queen Victoria Crown measuring about 5cm in diameter. We wanted a coin minted in 1897, because that was the foundation year of the VFL, later the AFL. On one side of this big, heavy coin was a large portrait of Queen Victoria's head, so there could never be any confusion about what side was heads. We had a dinner with Wayne Jackson and his wife, Liz, and Mark presented the coin to him in a special case. The intention was that the coin could be used in future grand finals. But the AFL had a contract with Coca Cola to use a particular coin.'

So, the previous year's grand final toss was swirling around in Mark's memory as he soaked up the pre-match atmosphere against North Melbourne. The ground almost rumbled with the noise and nervous energy of 94 431 supporters. Huge cliffs of people rose from the boundary line, a blurred patchwork of red, gold, blue and white. Running around the ground, it was like whizzing past a circle of people from a hurdy-gurdy and, somewhere in the middle, music was playing. The umpire called the Adelaide skipper and his opposing captain Wayne Carey in to toss the coin, another in the commemorative collection. Instantly, Mark asked which side was heads, and they agreed. Having called heads, he lost the toss.

Early in the game, Adelaide's defence – led by Hart, Caven, Bickley and Goodwin – held firm against the North Melbourne offensive. Carey had been a formidable presence in the opening minutes, but Caven began to find his measure. At quarter time, the Crows were eight points behind the premiership favourites. In the second term, North Melbourne threw everything in its armoury against the Crows, exerting enormous duress on the defence. Yet, the desperate Adelaide resistance forced errors on North players, who kicked 2.11 for the quarter. At the other end of the ground, the Crows had managed only 1.1. By half-time, North had 21 scoring shots to 7. They had recorded 34 more kicks than Adelaide and 14 more handballs. As a result of this abysmal kicking for goal – creating only a 24-point margin – North was assailable, particularly for a Crows side that had demonstrated its capacity to inch its way back into games against formidable odds.

Tanya had been uneasy. The previous year, pregnant with Natasha, she could not celebrate through the night with the other players and their wives and partners. This year, she had a free rein to enjoy herself. But something did not feel right. She was not alone in her trepidation. 'On grand final day, Di Reid, John's wife, put on a lunch at the Hilton Hotel for the girls. Patsy Blight got us all to sing the club song. It was our little tradition. But there was a really strange sensation. There was no nervousness, and none of us liked the feeling. We were frightened of feeling so confident. I'll always remember that I'd given up on them at half-time. But there was a little girl with beautiful, golden ringlets sitting in front of me, the daughter of our team runner, Peter Jonas. When I was down in the dumps after two quarters, she turned to me and said, "You know they always come back in the last half!"'

Malcolm Blight paced the floor, giving the players time to grasp the reality of the situation, to analyse themselves. Finally, the coach stopped pacing, and turned towards the team. Within the four walls was a psychological engine room in which Blight slowly turned the cogs of inspiration and the pistons of self-belief. In carefully measured words, he said, 'Look, if you don't put up an effort here, all the work you've done, and the fact that we are underdogs, won't matter. The media and the public will never let you off the hook for letting the opportunity slip without giving it everything you've got.'

The one prospect that had lifted the Adelaide Football Club off the rack during the year had been the possibility of humiliation; people saying that their first flag had been a freak, and that they had stolen a premiership against a side that was not a seasoned finalist. As Blight spoke, Mark felt the change in atmosphere. 'We started to look around and realise we had some hard-nosed competitors. That's when you get the belief . . . when it's pretty tight in games and everything is in the balance. You look around and believe that the players won't let it slip. We had blokes who weren't prepared to take second best, or to take backward steps. That's where the belief came from.'

When he had the collective mindset in order, Blight then worked on the battle plan, urging his players to be more attacking. In military terms, the outcome of a battle is determined by the ability of a commander to bring about a decisive manoeuvre. First, this involves gaining intelligence and knowledge about the movements and intentions of potential aggressors. Armed with that knowledge, the commander is then able to coordinate his forces to maximum operational effect. In the battle space of the MCG on grand final day in 1998, Malcolm Blight's decisive manoeuvre came about through switching Kane Johnson and Mark Bickley from defence to the midfield. He also brought Andrew McLeod into the centre and switched Darren Jarman to full forward.

Mark's match fitness had been improving gradually after a late season lay-off with a hamstring injury, and he welcomed the opportunity to be released from defence into a running role.

The pressure shifted in the third term as Shaun Rehn gained supremacy in ruck with Bickley and Johnson controlling the middle. Matthew Robran began to control the forward lines and, suddenly, McLeod and Jarman began to crack the game open. Time and time again, Adelaide surged forward, finally levelling the scores when Nigel Smart hit the post from a set shot deep in the forward pocket. There were ominous signs for North Melbourne as the Crows' confidence grew. Brett James and Mark Ricciuto seized every moment; Andrew Eccles, Peter Caven and Simon Goodwin dominated the defence, pushing the ball into attack. In the dying seconds of the quarter, Smart threaded the ball through the goals, turning a 24-point half-time deficit into a slender lead. It was, in the classic sense, a premiership quarter of football.

As James Thiessen kicked a goal after a brilliant interception from McLeod in the opening seconds of the final quarter, the Crows were bound for glory. The unthinkable was happening as North Melbourne, who had been heading for their 12th straight victory, began to chase. The hugely outnumbered Crows supporters began to rise in the grandstands, screaming in delight as Eccles, Goodwin,

Thiessen, Johnson, Bickley, McLeod and Jarman turned on the fireworks. North's grand expectations crashed from despair to misery with goals to Smart, Jarman, Smart again, then Vardy. The grand final that was supposed to be a funeral march for the precocious underdogs instead became a procession of delirious joy. It was raining goals in Melbourne and tears poured forth in Adelaide.

The game had been frenetic, passionate and explosive. But as North Melbourne succumbed to the Adelaide 'bombing raid', there was a rare opportunity to relax, even though it was only for a second or two. Peter Bell had kicked a point after a 50-metre penalty, and somebody behind the fence attempted to souvenir the ball. As it was being retrieved from the crowd – a crazy mixture of dumbstruck and delighted – Kane Johnson and Mark Bickley came alongside each other. They had been prime movers in an amazing last half revival. Everything seemed quiet, even the joyous chorus of Crows supporters in the grandstands seemed kilometres away.

Forlorn North Melbourne players dragged their feet. Wayne Carey's huge shoulders slumped. Everything seemed to be moving in slow motion. Johnson and Bickley, only metres apart, were bent over double, sucking in the air, exhausted, but ready to go again. Mark – 15 kicks, 7 handballs – looked over to the young gun: 14 kicks, 10 handballs. 'We were both bent down, hands on our knees. I turned to Kane and called out 'Sugar!' to attract his attention. He looked at me. It was the first time we'd made eye contact since half-time. I winked, as if to say, "We've got it mate!" He smiled back at me. It was a moment I'll never forget.'

The final score was 15.15 (105) to 8.22 (70). North Melbourne had not kicked a goal in the last quarter, managing only to continue its inexplicable inaccuracy with seven behinds. When the siren blew, the victorious team descended on two players – Mark Ricciuto and Peter Vardy. But there were so many heroes. Among them was

Caven, who backed his own judgement and broke the spirit of champion Wayne Carey. Andrew McLeod, another champion, won his second Norm Smith Medal. Darren Jarman kicked five goals. Lion-hearted Shaun Rehn rucked Adelaide into supremacy and Ben Hart blocked, ran and weaved and then delivered with such surety that North Melbourne could not crack the Crows' defence. Mark Stevens, who had once been a North Melbourne player, rejoiced in his own grand final performance for Adelaide. Malcolm Blight and Mark Bickley stood on the podium again and hoisted the greatest prize in football.

In Adelaide, it was a repeat of the previous year, but it was bigger. People sang longer and louder. The city was choked with revellers. Never, ever, ever again could Adelaide be accused of being a pretender. They had beaten a powerhouse of the AFL. On a smaller scale, but at the heart of the matter, the Adelaide rooms at the MCG were drenched with emotion. Tanya Bickley didn't cry, but Babs Bickley did. It was, without hesitation, one of the happiest occasions in Mark's life. A dual premiership captain, he was celebrating with the people who mattered most in his life – his family and his teammates.

As the crowd dispersed from the rooms, the coach and players wanted to repeat their pledge of the previous season. Soon after 6.30 pm on Saturday, 26 September 1998, they walked out onto the dark, silent bowl of the MCG and its twinkling surrounds for a photograph. Another picture for posterity; a debriefing without words. After the revelry in the rooms, awash as they were with beer and champagne, it had been time for showers. However, an explosion at the Esso Longford gas station had cut supply to much of Victoria, which meant freezing showers at the MCG. There was talk that two men had been killed in the explosion, and eight seriously injured. In the Crows' change rooms, it was a case of a daring 'in and out' shower for the most celebrated footballers in the nation before they dressed for the team photograph.

Sport is a great leveller, an arena in which you should expect the unexpected. After the picture was taken on the MCG, the players pledged to return in 1999, then boarded a bus for the celebration dinner. Mark recalls how the bus was stopped in its tracks.

'Everyone was on a high, especially Mark Stevens because he'd played so well against his old side. As we were leaving the MCG, this guy came running up and bashed on the side of the bus. He was screaming, "I've got to speak to Mark Stevens. I've got to speak to Mark Stevens!" Stevo spotted him and yelled to the driver to stop because the guy was his close mate. So we stopped the bus and the bloke said he had to tell Stevo what had happened, that his dad had been one of the men killed in the gas explosion. There was not a lot that we could do, but I guess it was his way of coping with the tragic news about his dad and he wanted to tell Stevo first-hand. So we went from a high to a deep low. It was such a levelling experience. We'd whinged about having a cold shower, but this bloke had lost his dad. You could have heard a pin drop for a while. Grand finals are so hugely important, but things like that put sport back into a clear perspective. I think, in our own way, we paid our respects, even if it was in our own silence. Then we went on to enjoy what we'd achieved.'

The celebration dinner at the World Trade Centre was a sensational event, and this time the players knew what to expect the next day when they flew home to Adelaide. During the night, Mark shared plenty of beers with his brother, David.

'My brother couldn't quite believe where this whole football thing had taken me,' Mark said. 'David knew – and I knew – that if he really had a crack at it, he could have gone a long way beyond his achievements in the Spencer Gulf League. David was a better player than me. He played with distinction in the country league and I captained an AFL side. But that was no measure of the difference in our abilities. I have no doubt my success can be sourced back to the competition I had with my brother when we were boys. Every ball I got was a lesson, and I can tell you it was from a school of hard knocks. He was highly competitive and it gave me a very determined outlook on life.'

Back in Adelaide, 40 000 people packed Wayville Showgrounds for the welcome-home party. The adoring fans had seized on Malcolm Blight's post-match observation that 'If you win one, that's great. If you win two, well, you're freaks. Three, and it's a miracle.'

Within hours of the Crows' second successive premiership, the supporters wanted another. They believed in miracles.

22

SOLDIERING ON

The success of the Adelaide Football Club began to take its toll on both the coach and the players. At first, it was not evident. But, on reflection, there were pressure points that compounded into problems that snowballed into dilemmas.

Due to their finals triumphs in 1997 and 1998, intense pressure consumed the month of September. There had to be time to relax – to allow the players to not only enjoy their achievements, but to regain their touch with reality. In late 1996, when Blight first arrived at the club, the players had 13 weeks of pre-season training to achieve a certain standard of fitness by Christmas. This was a crucial benchmark. In 1997, this period was reduced to ten weeks. In 1998 it was seven weeks. For the players and their coach, the workload was enormous and Mark believes it began to have an impact on them, both physically and mentally.

'By the end of 1998, there was a cumulative effect. This began to manifest itself in stress-related injuries. And we were up there to be knocked off. Teams really measured themselves against us. Any team that has success confronts this issue. Then, when you are on top, you have a personal expectation to stay there and, of course, so do the supporters. So there is added pressure.'

In December 1998, Malcolm Blight reportedly sat down with his old mate, John Reid, and confided in him that if he had the choice, he would have preferred to finish his term with the Adelaide Football Club at that point. He spoke of being tired and said he hoped that he would feel regenerated by the start of the 1999 season.

Blight had in fact, been in a position to determine his future after the Crows' second premiership. 'At the end of the 1998 season, it was my call about whether or not I continued as coach. During that season, Bill Sanders came to me because there had been some speculation about me going to another club. Bill said the Board was pretty keen for me to stay with Adelaide. I asked Bill to put off the discussion for a while. Eventually, he came back and said something like, "What about doing it for me?" Without being too flowery about it all, I said to Bill, "Look, I'll sign up for another two years just for old times' sake."' Blight also told Bill that if he reached a stage where he wanted to go, that there should be no encumbrance on him.

'I've known Bill for 40 years. I trust him, and hopefully he trusts me. It's funny because I had told Bill when I came to Adelaide that if a premiership cup just happened to jump on the mantelpiece, I was likely to bolt. I've got this thing inside me that says once you have done something, its time to move on. So, when Bill ran on to the MCG after the 1997 grand final win against St Kilda, his first words were, "Don't say anything about going, don't say anything." I went home and spoke to Patsy about it, and she said it would not be right to leave. She said it would look like I'd grabbed the lollies and run. I wouldn't like anyone to think that of me. I always want to feel that I have contributed. In the end, I said to Patsy, "That was a bit of fun. I wonder if we can do it again."'

So they did it again in 1998. But what was the longer-term cost of the back-to-back premiership? A cruel run of injuries, starting with

Shaun Rehn in the opening Ansett Cup game of the 1999 season. Mark recalls the dramatic circumstances. 'In the centre of the ground was a rubberised plate. It was flush to the soil so that when the umpires bounced the ball, there was a solid base. Rehnny came in and trod on the plate. He slid, then his sprigs hit the lush turf around the plate, jarring his knee and snapping the posterior cruciate ligament.'

The young guys, in particular, sustained a lot of soft-tissue injuries. Kane Johnson and Andrew Eccles began to suffer from what Mark perceived to be stress-related injuries. Mark twisted his ankle and missed four weeks, then he injured his collarbone. The combination of injuries meant that players could not attain a level of consistency.

Blight admits that by year three, he started to get sick of it all. 'We'd won another premiership, but a few days later we were back talking about players and planning another year. We had so many injuries. Usually, I just dismiss injuries and look for the next kid. But every week somebody was injured. I started to think it was not an even playing field. I started to query myself.'

Cracks began to appear in the coach's demeanour, and Mark believes the signs of duress were becoming increasingly evident. 'When we started having injury problems, there were signs of stress on the coach. We could see it. The beauty about Blighty was that he had never varied his coaching style. But there were a couple of occasions early in 1999 when he did step outside the set game plan. In the past, Blighty had been hard on players, but he had the ability to win them back after games. In that final year, I think he actually overstepped the boundary on a couple of occasions and things got a bit personal. He was passing some of his own stress on to the players, and a few of the guys were put out by it.'

John Reid describes it as chemistry – chemistry that worked beautifully for two years, before simply tapering off. 'Malcolm was knackered. He and Patsy are relatively private. Some people are happy to go to the pictures, to have everybody look at you and talk about you. But Malcolm would wait until it was dark, sneak into the theatre and leave before the movie finished because he wanted some privacy. The first premiership, then the second, put enormous demands and levels of expectation on him. I've known Malcolm for a long time, and I sensed he was starting to put demands and expectations on himself as a coach. He has always had the attitude of "Let's put things into place, do what we have to do and what will be will be." But I had not seen Malcom put pressure on himself like that before.

'Patsy became ill and I have no doubt that as much as Malcolm thought he was coping with that, it was a worry. Nothing went right, and it got him in the end. He ran out of petrol. I get very annoyed with people saying he walked out on us. They wouldn't know. My grandma used to say, "Don't be too critical until you wear someone else's slippers," and in my book, that's a fair call.'

It all came to a head on Wednesday, 14 July 1999 – the most dramatic day in the club's history. Blight announced his resignation in the afternoon, following a meeting with the players. In that emotional meeting, Mark feels it all started to make sense. 'Initially, the players were shocked. But then Blighty explained his reasons, saying he was running low on petrol and he was stressed out. He had tested the extremes of his capacity, but wasn't getting a result. It had just got the better of him. Looking back, we knew he had gone through some stressful times. He'd go really hard at us, then a week later he was exactly the opposite. In the end, he told us he'd been putting more effort into creating success than normal. When it didn't work, he decided to give it away.'

After a loss to Carlton, Blight had gone home and acknowledged he was not enjoying anything about football. He explains, 'There had been talk about Patsy being sick. She was fine by that time, although I had been concerned about her. I also had a virus or flu for about two months, and I felt terrible. I rang John Reid and told him I was struggling. I told him I was thinking about the future and that the club should do the same.

'There were a lot of dominoes, and they all seemed to fall the same way. I was bemused by some comments from members of the public who questioned my coaching and movement of players. Supporters sometimes have short memories. I was bloody tired and actually started listening to the criticism. It was then that I realised it was time to move on. I told the club that I would continue to coach through to the end of the 1999 season and that I would be totally professional about it. The fact is that the club made the decision to go on the front foot and announce it publicly before the end of the season.'

Meanwhile, the Crows had a game to play the following Saturday against the Western Bulldogs at the MCG. Club chairman, Bob Hammond, met with Mark and some of the other senior players to stress the importance of maintaining focus, and not letting the season drift away. He said a few of the younger players were going to be confused about the Blight situation, and it was the team leaders' job to keep them focused. Mark recalls the chairman's very steady hand on the tiller of the club. 'Bob had never interfered in the playing aspects of the club, but he spoke our language, and we had great respect for him. He had credibility as a former player and coach at SANFL and AFL level. He had an experienced background in the game, but he mostly kept it up his sleeve. When he did speak, it was worth pinning your ears back to listen because of his immense footy knowledge.'

The Crows threw everything at the Western Bulldogs on Saturday, 17 July. They were 47 points ahead at three-quarter time, but in the last term the Bulldogs overran their opponents and stole victory by two points. Mark described it as the most demoralising loss he could remember. The Crows won their next two games against Hawthorn and St Kilda, but lost the final four as the weary coach counted down the days. Adelaide finished the season in 13th position.

Incredibly, Blight now suggests that he could have been talked out of leaving the club to which he had brought so much success. 'After the announcement that I would be leaving at the end of the season, and that the club was looking for a new coach, Bob Hammond said to me, "Why didn't you finish the year and go away for four months, just to freshen up?" In hindsight, that was a pretty fair call. If that scenario had been put to me at the time, I might have continued with the Adelaide Football Club. But who knows.'

The reality, though, was that the coach had had enough. Mark applauds Blight's decision to put the club before himself. 'He could easily have gone another year . . . gone through the motions. But he felt it was more important for the club to have a new and passionate coach. Just before he left, I shared a bottle of wine with Malcolm and we talked about a lot of things. It was a chance for Malcolm Blight to have a yarn with Mark Bickley, not coach and captain. He was relieved it was over. He'd bought a house on the Gold Coast, and he just wanted to go up there and recharge his batteries.

'Blighty is a great bloke. There is a degree of mystique about him, but he really is a down-to-earth, likeable person. He loves footy and the history of the game. He was my footy hero as a kid, and to get to know him personally was a great privilege.'

Blight now reflects on his time at the Adelaide Football Club with a great deal of pleasure. 'My role was probably a cameo, in the true sense of the word. When the history of the Adelaide Football Club is written, Mark Bickley's name will be mentioned more than mine, and rightly so. Mark says he was the last player taken in 1991, and he has withstood everything and been through a lot.

'My time was great, but it was never going to be long for lots of reasons. If I could write my own epitaph, it would read something like, "Played at North Melbourne after they gave me an opportunity, and I also had an opportunity to coach at a very young age." In fact, I started coaching at a younger age than Mark is now.

'Somewhere deep down, people might like to be a Kevin Sheedy and coach at the one club for 20 years. But moving on has become a part of me, and I'm not disappointed about that. In the end, I just hope that I had some positive influence on some of the young players at the Adelaide Football Club. If I have done that, I have fulfilled what I set out to do.'

23

A NEW COACH, A NEW START

When Gary Ayres arrived, the Adelaide Football Club was in a state of metamorphosis. In football parlance, the goals had shifted. Stricken with injury, probably a degree of psychological fatigue, and the indefinable quirks of human nature, the club had fallen on hard times. There had been no significant changes in the management or playing staff. Indeed, it was the club's chief executive, Bill Sanders, who summed up the situation when he said that success should never be taken for granted. In the Crows Yearbook published at the start of the 2000 season, he stated in part: 'I really believe the club should benefit from the disappointment of last season, and we should learn from it. One of the things I found last year was that there was still this expectation among the public that, having won two premierships, it was going to happen again ... some people thought three in a row was just a matter of going around. Realistically, you know you're not going to finish top every year because the system won't allow it. The equalisation policy, which we support, is there to provide a balanced competition, so you're not going to get the domination of clubs.'

The Adelaide Football Club's objective in 2000 was to make the top eight. In selecting Gary Ayres as a successor to Malcolm Blight, the Crows recruited a person who was a decorated veteran of finals football. All things being equal, he could take them there again. During a 269-game career at Hawthorn from 1978 to 1993, he grew accustomed to playing in finals. His career included five premierships and two Norm Smith Medals, ample credentials for the AFL's Hall of Fame. He had also succeeded Malcolm Blight as coach of Geelong, taking the Cats into a grand final. He was Blight's apprentice at Geelong, but he was always his own man, and he was respected for it.

Mark Bickley also had the responsibility of leading the players out of the wilderness. He'd served two years as captain of a premiership side, and one year leading a team on a slippery dip. Serving a new coach in a club that had farewelled some of its veterans, including Rod Jameson, Matthew Liptak, David Pittman and Simon Tregenza, Mark faced a great test of character. He drew strength from Ayres, in whom he saw an iron-willed determination to succeed. 'The players held a deep respect for him. From the start, we could see that if he put his mind to something, he was like a dog with a bone. He is the sort of person who won't let it go until he achieves what he wants. It's easy to see why he was such a hard and competitive player.'

On 6 April 2000, the Port Pirie Regional Council sent a letter to the organisers of the Sydney Olympic Torch Relay. It read:

> *It is my pleasure to nominate Adelaide Crows captain Mark Bickley as a possible community torchbearer for the Sydney 2000 Olympic Torch relay for the following reasons:*
>
> *It is but once in a 100 years that an athlete makes an impact on a community, as has our favourite son, Mark Bickley;*

> Through his dedication, commitment and hard work, he was selected as captain of the Adelaide Crows, and led them to AFL premierships in 1997 and 1998;
>
> His achievements in the sporting arenas of Australia ensure his name is etched forever in Port Pirie's distinguished 150-year history. No person, either past or present, has ever made the people of the City of Friendly People so proud. He is our finest ambassador;
>
> Mark is a committed worker for a number of charities and is an ambassador for Child and Youth Health.
>
> It would be an inspiration to us all if he was chosen as a torchbearer.
>
> Yours sincerely
> Ken Madigan
> Mayor

Mayor Madigan also wrote to the Adelaide captain advising him of the nomination to carry the Olympic torch on a section of its winding journey through Port Pirie. Mark was overjoyed about the prospect of hoisting the flame for the Olympic ideal. The Olympic Games are the ultimate sporting threshold – the Everest of every athlete. Mark counted among his sporting heroes Steve Moneghetti and Kieren Perkins, marathon men on land and water. What he admired most about them was that despite scaling the highest mountains of personal endeavour, they greeted defeat and disappointment as necessary neighbours of glory and adulation. They were people of character. To participate in a small way in the amazing phenomenon of the Sydney Olympics was a fantastic proposition.

His nomination for the Olympic torch relay was not accepted. There was no explanation. There was disappointment, but no bitterness. 'I'd previously been presented with the keys to the City of Port Pirie, and lauded quite enough. But I would love to have carried the torch for my family. In November 1998, the Solomontown Footy Club staged a Bickley Family Appreciation Dinner. It was not about Mark Bickley. It was more a vote of thanks to the other members of the family, and the work they'd put in. Mum and Dad were involved from a very young age and David, like me, had been down at the club in a dressing gown since he was a little kid.'

Like his predecessors Chris McDermott and Tony McGuinness, Mark recognised that being captain of the Adelaide Football Club could be a unifying position and one of influence in the community, particularly in highlighting the plight of sick children. McDermott had met Nathan Maclean, who was diagnosed with a rare brain tumour. They formed a friendship that brought great happiness until Nathan died in February 1993. McGuinness met Nicholas Berry, who was battling kidney cancer. They also became close mates, keenly following each other's progress until medical science ran out of answers for the young boy in December 1994. The two former Crows captains were so touched by their experiences with these brave boys, they established a fundraising body – the McGuinness McDermott Foundation – in 1996 to help improve oncology treatment facilities for children in South Australia. Since then, hundreds of thousands of dollars have been raised to make life longer and easier for children with serious diseases.

Mark's first league coach, John Reid, regularly took the South Adelaide players to visit sick children. Mark recalls how such visits raised the spirits of the young people, and helped the players cope with tough times in football. 'In those days with South, we were downtrodden and struggling. But whenever we thought the world was caving in, John would take us into the Burns Unit or the Cancer Ward at the Adelaide Children's Hospital. To see the people in there and what their families were going through, left us humbled and appreciative of the fact that we had our health and well-being.

Later, whenever requests were made to the Adelaide Football Club to support sick people, we tried to help out.'

In 1998, Mark was appointed South Australia's first Ambassador for Child and Youth Health Services, supporting an organisation providing support facilities for people in need. 'The role has been about encouraging people and letting them know there are some great resources available to help them. Services like this need prominent people to push their work to the forefront, and if being involved helps to do that, I think it's great. It's been a privilege to be involved.'

During a visit to St Monica's Primary School in Adelaide in 2000, Mark's advocacy for young people took a new dimension: the schoolyard dilemma of bullying and peer group pressure. *The Southern Cross* newspaper reported on his visit to talk with the students about self-worth, and to farewell the Crows' crazy parish priest, Father Peter Milburn. The article read in part:

> *As a slightly built youngster growing up in the Iron Triangle smelting town of Port Pirie, Mark Bickley learned early the advantages of ducking and weaving his way out of strife. When that didn't work, or when he was singled out by bullies, he had his fail-safe fall-back – his older, bigger brother.*
>
> *'Sometimes, you feel you have to fit in to go along with the group,' he said in an interview at St Monica's Primary School. 'As you get older, you realise the most important thing is to be yourself. Kids don't have to try and be anything they aren't. They should just try to be themselves and people will like them for what they are.'*
>
> *His attitudes to peer group pressure and bullying, both in the schoolyard and on the playing field, set an example for young people faced with the 'cringe factor' – struggling on the fringes of the schoolyard, thirsty for acceptance and the*

elusive quest of 'cool'. Mark said because he had been a 'little kid at school', he had experienced bullying. 'But I was probably a bit smart – I tried not to get into that position.'

On the football field, he said while some players tried to intimidate others, 'the primary reason we're out there is to try to win the ball, play well and win the game. If you're worried too much about trying to intimidate players or bully them, you're taking your mind off the job. I've always been taught to think only about the game, and how you can get a kick rather than trying to put other blokes off their game.'

The Adelaide Football Club fell short of its objectives in 2000. After losing the first five games, the Crows recovered slightly and gave themselves a chance of making the final eight. But it was a season of inconsistency and bitter disappointment. The club finished in 11th position, with 9 wins and 13 losses. During the season, two players achieved their 200-game milestone – Nigel Smart and Mark Bickley. For the former, the game was a joyous occasion, for the latter, it was a day of disappointment. 'I won't forget Nigel's 200th game. It was against Richmond at Colonial Stadium, a really exciting game which we won by nine points. Nigel played well and we lifted him up and carried him off the ground. It was a game befitting his career. He is a unique character – a confident and creative footballer, talented in the air and on the ground. He is so smooth that sometimes people don't realise he's desperate. But he gives 100 per cent. Nigel is also a guy who thinks outside the square. He can question authority in a constructive sense, and I think people respect his point of view.'

Mark's 200th game – and his 100th as captain – was against Carlton at Optus Oval. Before the game, he said, 'Winning against Carlton is much more important than my 200th game. We are in a precarious position, but if this milestone can be part of the motivation for the team to win, that will be the reward for me.'

Adelaide lost by 24 points and Mark suffered serious ligament damage to his shoulder. 'We all trudged off the ground, heads down. But I was very humbled by all the cards, letters and good wishes I received before and after the game. It is especially nice when people put words on paper.'

Mark's greatest praise was for Tanya, who gave birth to Aleesha nine days after the Carlton game. 'When it all starts out, football is your number-one priority. Everything revolves around it. As you get older, especially when your own family comes along, your priorities change. Over the years, Tanya has made enormous sacrifices to enable me to keep football in the front of my mind. I have no doubt there is a correlation between a stable and steady environment off the field and a successful career on it, and I have to thank Tanya enormously for her support.'

The letters and articles of congratulations on Mark's 200-game milestone were extraordinary in their diversity. These are excerpts from just a few:

> *On behalf of the AFL Commission, I would like to pass on our sincere congratulations and best wishes. It is a magnificent achievement and a fitting milestone in becoming only the second player in the history of the Adelaide Football Club to reach 200 games. Your courage, leadership and passion for the game has not only won you respect in your home State of South Australia. All over the country, you are admired as one of the great leaders in AFL football ... You are a wonderful role model and ambassador for the game.*
>
> Wayne Jackson
> Chief Executive Officer, Australian Football League

> *I am writing to congratulate you on behalf of all players, coaches, members and supporters of the South Adelaide Football Club ... Certainly within the South Adelaide zone*

of the SANFL, it is a great advantage to be able to point out to young players and their parents that Mark Bickley played his early years of league football with the club, demonstrating what is possible for players aspiring to play at the highest level. I am also sure that you have provided great inspiration to people outside of the football world as a family man and a person who is achieving success in the business world.

Stuart Palmer,
Chairman, South Adelaide Football Club

Heartiest congratulations on achieving your latest milestone. Throughout your career, you have been a credit to your family, yourself and the game of Australian football.

Ken Jeffrey
President, Spencer Gulf Football League

I have deliberately steered clear of proclaiming my utmost respect and admiration for your ongoing achievements, as I have wanted to be viewed as a friend, rather than a fan. However, I am unashamedly one of your fans who has followed your professional and personal achievements with great pride and respect. When achieving a milestone, I think you should take the time to reflect on the past and look towards the future. For me, two aspects of your career come immediately to mind.

Your first game when you carried the ball the length of the outer wing, then some. I remember you saying afterwards your adrenalin was racing as the crowd rose with you. While I didn't tell you at the time, my adrenalin was racing with you because I could tell you were going to be there to stay.

The look on your face after the 1997 grand final. Knowing you well, it was an experience for me to see the look of unbridled joy on your face and to understand, in part, your emotions at that stage.

Looking to the future, the speculation among the media throng about your future has already started. The day will come when a kick and a catch will no longer be carried out in anger.

I draw on an interview Roy and HG had with Evander Holyfield. When the boys asked Evander about retirement in a manner akin to asking him about the death of a loved one, he responded with a stunned look on his face. 'My life does not end when I retire. I have a beautiful family and my sport has provided me with a wonderful springboard for the start of my life.'

Jason, Janette, Jake and Ellie Turner

From those early days of our first meeting in Max and Babs's kitchen; the fun and mateship at the Solly rooms in the corner with Pinky; Monday night teas with your family and the card games after; your first games . . . For all of us who have followed your career from the start, you have given us great pleasure and pride . . . Your honesty, determination and courage can never be questioned. Play Fos Williams's way and you will never fail. Courage above all.

Bob, Gaynor, Elizabeth and Henry Boston

Bicks, Skipper, Skippy Pick Your Bum, Bazz, Most Popular Guy In The Place Tonight etc etc

Congratulations on the 200. Every one of them has been memorable. I will never forget your courage, leadership, determination, but mostly the friendship that we enjoyed as teammates. Wish I was there.

Matthew Liptak

Football writers and commentators were equally complimentary. Perhaps it was Tommy Hafey who best summed up the sentiments of the media when he wrote: 'The captain doesn't just lead his team onto the field and toss the coin. He is the role model for the others, the coach's right-hand man on the field, and the first and best at following all the team rules and disciplines. He is the on-field cheer leader. His honesty and loyalty and his desperation with every single issue must never waver. He must be respected for his actions and his image with his teammates, the people at the club and the thousands of supporters who not only follow the Crows, but all supporters of our great game. Mark Bickley qualifies in all areas. I don't know anybody who hasn't been won over by the way he has presented himself with his fantastic attitude.'

Late in the 2000 season, former Chairman of Selectors John Halbert, former Team Manager Neil Kerley, selector David Marshall, club chairman Bob Hammond, Football Operations Manager John Reid and Chief Executive Bill Sanders selected Adelaide's team of the decade. Among those first selected were Malcolm Blight as coach, duel Norm Smith Medallist Andrew McLeod and captains Mark Bickley, Chris McDermott and Tony McGuinness. Mark was named Team Man of the Decade, a decision that was never challenged. On learning of the honour, Mark told *Advertiser* journalist Michelangelo Rucci, 'I think everyone who plays football wants to be thought of as a great team man – that when it comes to doing it for the team, they can do it. I can't kick, mark or handball. I was not going to kick a lot of goals or take the hangers. But I made sure I worked hard on the other parts of my game – tackling, smothering and giving the best I could. It was always going to be that way with my stature and capabilities. So this is a great honour.'

24

THE RIGHT TIME

The thought surfaces and disappears as if in the ebb and flow of a tide. But even when it is consumed by the swirling flood of distraction or exposed in sharp, undeniable corners of reality, the thought is constant. It prowls. The timing must be right. It must be a natural progression, a bit like osmosis. For four years, Mark had been captain of the Adelaide Football Club. Was it time to step down? Yes! No! Yes! Imagine the agony, anguish and uncertainty of this decision. Imagine, on the other hand, the pleasure of the transition; the border-crossing of responsibility. Mark describes it in intimate detail, but in the first instance it is worth recounting the matter-of-fact thoughts of John Reid, a trained observer and profound thinker in the game of football.

'When Mark stepped down as captain at the end of 2000, he simply stated the facts. Mark knows that a captain is required to do more work during the week and off the ground, particularly in a rebuilding stage. He summed it up well – not to be a hero, but simply facing reality. He had three little kids and a business to run. He was over 30, and he said it was time for a new leadership group.

Factual, realistic commonsense. His decision to step down as captain reflected his qualities as a person.'

One of Mark's clearest memories was at the end of the 1997 grand final. On the victory lap of the MCG, David Pittman lifted him into the air. Hoisting the premiership cup above his head, he stole a line from the hit movie *Titanic* and screamed: 'I'm the king of the world!' But, stepping back from the emotion of the moment, there was a player who always put the team before himself. He was a captain who said there were a handful of others in the side who would have been more than capable leaders. His own captaincy over four years, including two premierships, had been outstanding for its exemplary courage, tenacity and team play. But, at the end of 2000, he recognised it was time to fulfil the leadership ambitions and credentials of others in the same way that Malcolm Blight had opened the door for him in 1997.

Mark elaborates on the events leading up to his decision to step down. 'The season had been disappointing from a team and personal perspective, and the day after our last game, which we lost to Port Adelaide, I had a pretty serious talk with Mark Ricciuto. I didn't want to stand in the way of the next generation of leaders in the club, and I felt that Roo was ready to be captain. I wanted to ask Roo about the role, and he said he was bursting to do it. He was capable and ready. There were three or four other guys, including Ben Hart, Simon Goodwin and Andy McLeod, who were shaping up as leaders within the team. Nigel Smart and I had served our time. We were going to be steady, but we weren't going to be the matchwinners. Each of the up-and-coming leaders had played a lot of footy. They'd been All Australians and won club best and fairest awards. They were looking for other things in their footy careers to aspire towards. Leadership was the next challenge.'

Mark's young family and business commitments were also a major consideration. 'As captain, I always felt I had to be the first person at the club and the last person to leave. By relinquishing the captaincy, it made things a little easier for me. Coupled with that is the fact that as you get older, you start to think about how things will unfold in terms of form and injury. I didn't want to be in a position where I was captaining the club and not performing well. I had also discussed the situation with Tanya. She really thought I could go on doing it, but said she would support my decision, whichever way it went.

'The day after I talked things over with Mark Ricciuto, we had a get-together with the guys. I picked up Nigel Smart that morning, and in the car he said, "Look, I've got a letter here to give to Reidy this morning. It's my resignation as vice-captain, and I thought I'd better tell you first." You could have knocked me over with a feather. Then I told Nigel that I was going to resign, too. We had independently arrived at the same decision – that it was time for the younger guys to take over. We recognised that the younger leadership group was more in touch with what was happening in the team. Nigel and I were married with kids, and we didn't really get out much after the games. The younger guys would be a bit more accountable to Mark Ricciuto because he'd know what they were up to between games. It was all part of team dynamics.'

Having made his decision, Mark sought a meeting with Gary Ayres. 'He was a bit surprised, but he supported me when I explained my reasons. I think succession planning is part of being a good leader. I told Gary that if the younger guys were going to be entrusted with the responsibility of leadership, it made a lot of sense for Nigel and me to be playing with them to make the transition a bit easier, rather than being cast in at the deep end. I told Gary I was looking forward to playing and providing support in 2001. As it turned out, I have let the guys run their own race. I've offered advice and opinions, but only when I've been asked. The new leaders are now shaping the future of the club.'

Succession planning. Mark had begun to look over the horizon. But, first, there was the challenge of maintaining his own high standards on the field. 'There is a huge pride factor. If you're recognised as being a good player, you really want to make sure you continue that form. When you start out in this game, you want to be part of a team, being with your mates, playing footy and enjoying success. I was privileged to be captain of two premiership sides, but I am sure every player in the 1997 and 1998 sides enjoyed it as much as I did. I was quite happy in 2001 to be one of the players along the line, so long as I was contributing to the success of the club.'

Knowing when to retire is one of the hardest decisions an elite athlete has to face. Retirement can bring relief for a body screaming for mercy, the crossing of a proverbial equator into a new hemisphere of calmness and tranquillity – far from the biting chill of the training track and crunch of the contest. But retirement can also create a brooding emptiness, particularly for those who have not realised their greatest ambitions, or for whom the primary purpose of play was the adulation of their feats.

Few people could doubt the champion qualities of Tony Lockett of St Kilda and Sydney. Upon his retirement, Lockett said he counted himself extremely lucky to have achieved what he did in football – a Brownlow Medal, Coleman Medals, a Whitten Medal, best and fairest awards, and playing in the 1996 grand final. 'However,' he said, 'at the end of the day, I would gladly give up each and every one of them if I could only climb football's Everest and win a premiership. After 17 seasons in the VFL/AFL, that remains my one regret, not to have won a premiership. I've always loved football, but I've also loved winning and the ultimate win in football can only be a premiership.'

Mark obviously counts his blessings. 'Being in premiership sides means so much to me, but the greatest thing I've received from the game and the club has been the forging of lifelong friendships. I've been lucky to meet so many terrific people. A lot of people play football for a long time and never play in a premiership team. But they will always have their mates, and that's so important.'

Mark's time at the top has been long and sustained, commanding a position in the team whenever he has been available. Indeed, his playing record is remarkable. Since being elevated into the A-grade side as a 16-year-old with Solomontown, then on to South Adelaide and the Crows, Mark has never been dropped. He has missed games through injury, but he has always come straight back in the senior side.

During 2001, Mark resisted the thought for as long as he could, focusing instead on the fortunes of the football club in its second year under Gary Ayres. But, occasionally, he reflected on the careers of others and pondered. 'It's easy for people to say that somebody has played a year too long, particularly once a season has started. I think about Chris McDermott in his last year. If he had a crystal ball and had been able to look forward and see that he wasn't going to play that well and suffer injuries at the wrong time, he probably would have been the first bloke to retire at the start of the season. Everyone's vision is 20:20 in hindsight. Imagine if Craig Bradley had suffered a serious injury at the age of 33, missed four or five weeks and then had a couple of bad comeback games. People would say, "Gee, he's played a season too long, he should have retired last year." But, as it happens, Craig has been able to maintain his form and make a huge contribution for another four or five years. His style of play has allowed him to do that, and the same could be said of another great champion, Michael Tuck. On the other hand, there are footballers such as John Worsfold, who played a high-collision game. He retired before he was 30 because his body couldn't take it anymore.

'My motivation has always been getting the best out of myself. I don't want to die wondering what would have happened if I had done this? Or what would the result have been if I did that? Personal pride is a motivating thing for me and it's wrapped up in my performance. I'd hate to think that a supporter paid good money to go to a game and at the end hear him say, "I don't reckon Bickley had a go." I hope that nobody could ever say that about me.'

Chris McDermott, the Crows' first captain and the person who had such a significant influence on Mark's football life, describes him as one of game's most courageous players. 'It might only happen once in a game, or once in a season, but there comes a time when a player has to make a sacrificial act for the team without personal consideration. Mark Bickley does that without fear or hesitation. It's what made him such a great captain and team player, because he set examples for others and inspired the best in them. Knowing Mark as well as I do, I am sure his intention was to hand over the reigns of captaincy, then stay for a period to guide and support when needed. At the same time, he continued to play outstanding football. Mark has exceeded everything he set out to achieve in football. His job is complete and he should have no regrets. He has a wonderful life to go to outside the game, including his family, his business and the media.'

In July 2001, Mark and Tanya sat down to talk about bittersweet memories, and counted themselves extremely lucky. There had been sacrifices, though. 'People stopped asking us out to dinners and parties years ago because they knew that most often we couldn't go,' Tanya mused. 'Mark has been with the Crows since he was 21 and we've missed weddings, engagements and birthdays because he's been away playing. We have to plan dinner dates with friends three or four months in advance. There are a lots of things that people take for granted.'

So they began to seriously think about the football afterlife.

25

BACK FROM THE BRINK

Season 2001 ended for the Adelaide Football Club with a potent mixture of expectation and emotion; nostalgia, melancholy and despair. In there also was embarrassment. On the MCG – twice the ground of glory for the Crows – there was nowhere to hide after the dismal elimination final thumping by Carlton. The season had been a roller coaster ride and, despite a shock loss to Fremantle in the last minor round game, the Crows finished eighth and expected to have a big influence against the top sides in the finals.

For coach Gary Ayres – the fearless, dependable former Hawthorn defender who twice won the Norm Smith Medal for being best on ground in grand finals; who played in eight grand finals for five premierships; who in 1988 refused to leave the grand final arena against Melbourne despite a depressed fracture of the cheekbone; who coached Adelaide with the doctrine of accountability; and who sought a rightful place in the finals for his club after it finished in eleventh position the previous year – the 2001 finals series was not only the culmination of a lot of hard work, but the opportunity for the Crows to regain the respect they deserved. It didn't happen!

Instead the club made an inglorious exit against Carlton, thrashed by a side it had beaten twice during the year. The Adelaide fans were speechless. The club's hierarchy searched for explanations. Some of the players were in tears, including Darren Jarman. His final AFL game on the field of dreams was a disaster and an enormous personal disappointment. He deserved better.

Less than a fortnight earlier, Mark had agreed to play for another year after numerous approaches from the Adelaide Football Club. Despite having played his most consistent football for almost a decade, he had been committed to retirement. He admitted: 'I was sore and grumpy after some games, no doubt about that. I had to commit my body a lot in games; more frequently than in other years.'

The Round 18 loss to Port Adelaide at Football Park, a showdown that was crucial to the Crows' finals chances, was a significant milestone on Mark's road to retirement. His body ached unforgivingly after the game, and he was angry that the club had squandered a match-winning lead against the arch enemy. Then to make matters worse he was reported for charging. Twice before in his career, Mark had been cited by umpires for allegedly playing outside the rules of the game. In 1992, he received a one-match suspension for an illegal tackle against Footscray's Nigel Kellett, creating a vacancy in the team for a youngster called Ben Hart to play his first AFL game. In 1999, he was forced to sit out another week after being found guilty of striking Melbourne's Ben Beams. The report for charging Port Adelaide's Josh Carr left him frustrated and downcast. 'There were lots of reasons for feeling low after that game. I was particularly disappointed about being reported. Football is a game of split-second decisions. I was sprinting for the ball, and at the last second realised that I was not going to get there before the opposition player. I just had to make myself compact to avoid getting hurt.' The tribunal agreed and dismissed the charge.

Tanya Bickley was best placed to witness the battering Marks body had taken during 2001, and to understand the toll the tough season had on his mind. 'After the Port game, he came home exhausted and he was in pain. I'd never seen him look so down. Natasha ran up and gave him a cuddle and he said: "Oh, I needed that." Then he was reported for charging. He told me he didn't need it any longer. He'd had enough. Physically and emotionally, he was completely zapped. He was grumpy a lot of times during the season. Usually before a game nothing would bother him. The kids could be playing up, or I could be tired and a bit short-tempered. But usually he took it all in his stride. Before most games in 2001, everything bothered him. Our home became consumed with each match, and Mark's build up for it. It was getting worse, and I had almost had enough. There was this tension before a game, then afterwards he'd be exhausted. In the end, we had a bit of a talk about his attitude. I told him: "Look, if you're playing on, you'd better clean up your act because I'm not going to put up with this for another season." That might sound selfish, but we have three kids to care about.

'It has been pretty confusing. We were all set for Mark to retire. We even planned a holiday and looked forward to catching up with friends outside football every weekend. You have a love–hate relationship with football and sometimes you just want it to end. Every now and again throughout the season I'd ask Mark if he still planned to retire and he'd say: "Yeah, yeah." Perhaps, I should have known better.'

After losing to Port Adelaide, the Crows strung together three victories against Carlton at Football Park, the Kangaroos at Colonial Stadium and Hawthorn at Football Park. The trifecta secured Adelaide's position in the finals and a new mood prevailed in the club – a mood that enticed and prevailed upon the man who had twice led the Crows to premierships. The hunt for Mark's commitment for another year had, of course, started weeks before. Midfield coach Neil Craig kept urging him to get retirement out of his mind. At training, he prodded him with comments such as:

'Come on Bickley, you're not ready to retire yet.' After the win against Carlton in Round 19, Craig told Mark not to underestimate his worth in the Crows' midfield. John Reid, the Football Operations Manager at the Adelaide Football Club – effectively the player's manager – was more to the point. Reid called Mark and his manager Ian Gray into his office and told them the club wanted the name Bickley on the player list for 2002.

Reid had originally lured Mark out of Port Pirie to play for South Adelaide, and he has been with his recruit for most of his football career. He is forthright in his opinion of Mark's place in the history of the Adelaide Football Club. 'In footy terms, and off field, I don't think there has been anybody better,' he said. 'We've had better players, but I personally don't think there has been a better captain or role model for our footy club. I say that with great sincerity, and I say it with a fair degree of knowledge and understanding of what footy clubs are all about, and what people are required to do to make a club successful. It is not intended to be detrimental to anybody else, but I personally don't think there has been a better role model or contributor to our football club.'

Mark found himself in a quandary. 'The comments from Reidy and Neil Craig started to make me think seriously about playing on for another year. I told Tanya I was getting a big wobbly about the retirement thing. She said I should speak to some people about it.' The first person Mark called was his Dad. Max Bickley, a sound student of the game, was positive. He told his son he still had something to offer the club and the game, but only if he really wanted – in his heart of hearts – to play another season.

Gary Ayres had played his hand smartly, allowing Mark room to make up his own mind. He approached him briefly suggesting a chat when the time was right. After beating the Kangaroos at Colonial Stadium on Round 20, Mark considered the time had arrived. Firstly, he approached captain Mark Ricciuto and Simon Goodwin, two players he respected enormously. When Mark told them he was considering retirement, their response was blunt, emphatic and wrapped up in one word: 'Bullshit.' Ricciuto and Goodwin then worked hard to convince Mark to keep playing.

As the Adelaide touring party waited in Melbourne Airport's Golden Wing lounge after the game against the Kangaroos, Mark approached the coach. Ayers spoke of his own retirement from Hawthorn after the 1993 elimination final loss to Adelaide, knowing in his body and mind that his time was up. He told Mark his form and fitness were not in question, proposing his experience would be good for team balance in 2002.

Mark returned to Adelaide to tell Tanya. But she already knew. 'Towards the end of the season, the team was playing well and Mark's form had picked up,' she said. 'At one stage, I asked Mark how everything was going at the club and he suggested that he may play again in 2002. I realised that he was seriously considering delaying his retirement. Mark said there was a different atmosphere within the club and everybody was feeling confident. It was the happiest I'd seen him all year.

'The club had been chatting to him and saying nice things about his form. Despite some bad downers, I don't think Mark was ready to retire. The club really came after him for another season, and in the end I could see he wanted to play. It was still in his system. It was a very confusing time, and in a way I guess I was disappointed. I remember sitting up in the middle of the night rocking Aleesha in the chair and I thought to myself: "No, he can forget about football and start thinking about our future." But by morning I'd mellowed. I knew he had to play on and I will support him all the way. I am sure if he retired at the end of 2001, he'd regret it. He had to get it out of his system, and I'd hate to think I was the one who pushed him to retire prematurely.

'It's also important to remember that Mark is the absolute blueprint team man. His decision to play another season was as much about the team as it was for himself. I think in a way he decided to give something back for the loyalty the Adelaide Football Club has shown him over the years. At the same time, Mark is totally loving and loyal to his family, and I know there will be lots of time to do the things we plan when he finally retires.'

This account of Mark Bickley's life to date, revolving as it does around a game that means so much to Australians and the Australian character and identity, has been illuminated by the willing commentary of people who have played, coached or worked with him. After Mark publicly announced his intention to play again in 2002, ending intense media speculation, Gary Ayres was prompt with his praise. 'Mark Bickley is one of the most respected footballers in Australia,' he said. 'He is extremely professional on and off the field, a solid citizen and a wonderful ambassador for the club – qualities you would expect from an outstanding leader. In 2001, he relinquished the captaincy to Mark Ricciuto because he felt the club's future was best in the hands of a new and younger leadership group. He put the club before himself and that's the way he plays. In the hard passages – the smothers, the tackles and shepherds – you'll find Mark Bickley, totally fearless. I was keen for Mark to play another year because somebody of his calibre is good for team dynamics. He has the ability to relate to younger players and they can learn a lot from Mark. At the end of the day, the decision to play in 2002 was his and, as a realist, he had to judge whether he was physically and mentally up to the challenge. Having made up his mind, I know he will give it his absolute best.'

After releasing the burden of uncertainty about his future, Mark looked forward to finals success in September 2001. The elimination final loss to Carlton dashed his hopes, but it reinforced for him that he had made the right decision to continue playing. In the change rooms after the Carlton game, he looked across to see Darren Jarman in tears, cupping his face in his hands. 'We let him down,' Mark said. 'Darren was a sublime footballer, the Rolls Royce, the person who tore apart St Kilda and the Kangaroos with his skills in the 1997 and 1998 grand finals. Yet, his last game for the club ended on such a sour note. We were all pretty emotional. I would hate to think it was my last game and that it had ended in this way.

'It was a bitter end to 2001, but we have to look ahead and I believe the future is promising. In Malcolm Blight's last season as coach, we finished thirteenth. Gary Ayres has taken us to eleventh and eighth. There has been a transition of leadership within the club with people like Mark Ricciuto, Ben Hart, Simon Goodwin and Andrew McLeod at the helm. They command respect. Under the new leaders of the club, we have the mid-range players who know what the game is all about and who are looking to consolidate themselves as hard-nosed, consistent footballers. Under them are the long-term players, including Robert Shirley, Tyson Stenglein and James Gallagher.

'The whole journey with the Adelaide football club has been a privilege for me. I am honoured to be part of the club and to be counted as a team mate. I know that eventually my time will come and it will leave a big hole in my life. I envisage it will be like that feeling on the MCG after winning a grand final. You don't want to get off the oval. You want to soak up the atmosphere. You want it to last forever.'

www.ingramcontent.com/pod-product-compliance
Lightning Source LLC
Chambersburg PA
CBHW022049290426
44109CB00014B/1039